FIESCO'S CONSPIRACY AT GENOA

Fiesco's Conspiracy at Genoa

By Friedrich Schiller

*Translated by Flora Kimmich,
with an Introduction and Notes to the Text
by John Guthrie*

http://www.openbookpublishers.com

Translation © 2015 Flora Kimmich.
Introduction and Notes to the Text © 2015 John Guthrie

This work is licensed under a Creative Commons Attribution 4.0 International license (CC BY 4.0). This license allows you to share, copy, distribute and transmit the work; to adapt the work and to make commercial use of the work providing attribution is made to the author (but not in any way that suggests that they endorse you or your use of the work). Attribution should include the following information:

Friedrich Schiller. *Fiesco's Conspiracy at Genoa*. Translated by Flora Kimmich, with an Introduction and Notes to the Text by John Guthrie. Cambridge, UK: Open Book Publishers, 2015. http://dx.doi.org/10.11647/OBP.0058

In order to access detailed and updated information on the license, please visit http://www.openbookpublishers.com/isbn/9781783740420#copyright

Further details about CC BY licenses are available at http://creativecommons.org/licenses/by/4.0/

All links were active at the time of publication unless otherwise stated.

Digital material and resources associated with this volume are available at http://www.openbookpublishers.com/9781783740420#resources

ISBN Paperback: 978-1-78374-042-0
ISBN Hardback: 978-1-78374-043-7
ISBN Digital (PDF): 978-1-78374-044-4
ISBN Digital ebook (epub): 978-1-78374-045-1
ISBN Digital ebook (mobi): 978-1-78374-046-8
DOI: 10.11647/OBP.0058

Cover image: Bernhard Neher (der Jüngere), 'Die Verschwörung des Fiesco zu Genua' (fresco), photograph by Rolf-Werner Nehrdich, courtesy of the Zentralinstitut für Kunstgeschichte München/Rolf-Werner Nehrdich, Munich.

All paper used by Open Book Publishers is SFI (Sustainable Forestry Initiative) and PEFC (Programme for the Endorsement of Forest Certification Schemes) Certified.

Printed in the United Kingdom and United States by Lightning Source for Open Book Publishers

Contents

Introduction *John Guthrie*	vi
Fiesco's Conspiracy at Genoa *Translated by Flora Kimmich*	1
Act One	7
Act Two	33
Act Three	63
Act Four	83
Act Five	103
Notes to the Text *John Guthrie*	123
Select Bibliography	129

Portrait of Friedrich Schiller (between ca.1786 and ca.1791) by Anton Graff.
Oil on canvas. Dresden State Gallery.[1]

---

1   Image in the public domain, from Wikimedia Commons. See http://commons.wikimedia.org/wiki/File:Anton_Graff_-_Friedrich_Schiller.jpg

Introduction

'My *Robbers* may perish! My *Fiesco* shall remain.'[2]

The Conspiracy of Fiesco at Genoa was Schiller's second play and the first in which he dealt with a historical subject. After the *succès de scandale* that *The Robbers* (1781) had been, Duke Karl Eugen of Württemberg restricted Schiller's movements and he busied himself with finishing his medical dissertation to qualify as a doctor. The dissertation contains a reference to the historical figure of Fiesco, whom Schiller links with Catiline as an example of an extreme character who is led by his senses and passions. The same two figures are again linked on the title page of the play through a quotation from Sallust. Schiller was pointed in the direction of a particular view of the historical figure by Rousseau, who gives Fiesco as an example of the type of the sublime criminal.[3] He turned to historical accounts of Fiesco's conspiracy, but was not interested in adhering to all the historical facts: what fascinated him was a character whose moment of greatest success revealed his weakness and failure. He sensed that his play would more than challenge his audience, and as

---

2 'Meine *Räuber* mögen untergehen! Mein Fiesco soll bleiben.' Schiller, while working on *Fiesco*, as reported by Karl Philipp Conz. Quoted in Friedrich Schiller, *Werke und Briefe*, 12 vols. (Frankfurt 1980-2004) (abbreviated as WB), vol. 2 *Dramen I*, ed. Gerhard Kluge (Frankfurt 1988), p. 1182. I am grateful to Alessandra Tosi, Flora Kimmich and Charlotte Lee for their comments on an earlier version of this introduction, to Francis Lamport, whose translations of Schiller and infectious enthusiasm for Schiller's dramas on stage have long been a source of inspiration, and finally to Charles Freeman for a guided tour of Genoa in September 2014.

3 Schiller read Helfrich Peter Sturz, *Denkwürdigkeiten von Johann Jakob Rousseau*, Erste Sammlung (Leipzig 1779). See pp. 145-146.

with *The Robbers*, he wrote a preface and a further explanatory text that was posted up with the cast list for the first performance in Mannheim. He had a disheartening experience when he read from his play to actors from the Mannheim theatre and they showed no great interest. This was ascribed to his fierce declamatory style and strong Swabian accent. The one-man show was apparently not a good advertisement for staging the play, and this is understandable in view of the plenitude of characters involved, the use of masks and frequent changes of scene. The theatre intendant in Mannheim, Freiherr von Dalberg, was unimpressed and did not immediately offer Schiller the contract he was hoping for. The actor August Wilhelm Iffland, sitting on the same committee judging plays in Mannheim, certainly thought the play had weaknesses. But he also believed that it had great merits and was worth performing. After the play was published in spring 1783, Schiller created a stage version based on some of the suggestions made by Iffland. When the play was performed in Mannheim it was not the success that Schiller had hoped for. He attributed this to the political mentality of his audience: he said he thought there was not enough enthusiasm for republican ideas in the region.[4]

More success greeted a version of Schiller's play created by Karl Martin Plümicke in Berlin in 1784 and performed widely at other German theatres in the following years. Plümicke adapted the play to the audience's conservative taste – the revolutionary content is marginalised, the issue of freedom in Genoa and the future of the Republic disappears, monarchy is restored and Fiesco, a much nobler character here, whom both Verrina and Julia fail to kill, renounces his newly acquired ducal status and passes it to the eighty-year-old Andrea Doria before committing suicide.[5] Plümicke's tampering with the play may have been a reason why Schiller decided to make more changes to his own play and create a version for the stage, which was performed in theatres in Dresden and Leipzig. It shows Fiesco being stabbed by Verrina at the play's conclusion, though Schiller did not

---

4   Schiller's letter to his later brother-in-law W. F. H. Reinwald, 5 May 1784. Schiller, Friedrich von, *Schillers Werke*. Nationalausgabe. Ed. Julius Petersen et al. 42 vols. (Weimar: Herman Böhlaus Nachfolger, 1943-) . Vol. 23, p. 277.

5   See Liselotte Blumenthal, 'Aufführungen der Verschwörung des Fiesko zu Genua zu Schillers Lebzeiten (1783-1805),' *Goethe. Neue Folge des Jahrbuchs der Goethe-Gesellschaft* 27 (1995), 60-90; here pp. 75-78.

himself approve this ending. Schiller's play, in Plümicke's version and versions authorized by Schiller, was performed a number of times during his lifetime, but its popularity did not last. A critic in the *Journal des Luxus und der Moden* suggested in 1792 that plays like *The Robbers* and *Fiesco*, in which rebellion and uprising are directly shown, should for the present, when so much was subject to misunderstanding, not be presented on stage.[6] Once the radical phase of the French Revolution had set in, the taste for revolutionary plays in Germany died out and plays which dealt with republics became unpopular. Thus, even though the play does not have a clear political message, it was considered to be dangerous.

It is thought that Schiller got to know more about the subject of Fiesco's conspiracy in 1780 with reading Robertson's history of the reign of the Emperor Charles V of Spain.[7] Robertson as a Scottish Enlightenment historian was keen to show progress in history. He depicted Fiesco's conspiracy as one of the boldest actions in history and Fiesco as a noble, gifted and charismatic figure whose positive qualities shown in public yet masked deeper and darker ambitions.

He saw Fiesco as an inscrutable figure who was given to the pursuit of pleasure. His succinct description of the conspiracy was itself based on a detailed account of the events by Cardinal de Retz, which Schiller also studied.[8] Retz's *La Conjuration de Fiesque* (written in 1638-39) was in turn a bold adaptation of a narrative by the Italian historian Agostino Mascardi. The cautious political orthodoxy and the moral strictures of Mascardi are turned on their head by the young Abbé de Retz, who instead writes an enthusiastic apology for his Genoese hero's rebellion against the tyranny of the Dorias.[9] In de Retz's depiction of Fiesco, one can detect the idea of the hero as a pre-destined being. His rebellion against authority is motivated by a kind of inner conviction, a personal necessity that drives him to seek *gloire* at any cost.[10]

---

6 Quoted in WB 2, p. 1174.
7 A German translation of Robertson's *History* had been published in 1770-1771, and a second edition in 1779: *Dr. William Robertsons Geschichte der Regierung Kaiser Carls des Fünften. Aus dem Englischen übersetzt ... von Julius August Remer*, 3 vols. (Braunschweig 1770-1771). See G. Kluge, Commentary to WB 2, p. 1149.
8 *Des Kardinals von Retz Histoire de la conjuration du comte Jean Louis de Fiesque* (Paris 1682).
9 Derek Watts, *Cardinal de Retz. The Ambiguities of a Seventeenth-Century Mind* (Oxford 1980), p. 134.
10 Watts, pp. 135-136.

Portrait of Fiesco from Schiller's 1859 edition of *Die Verschwörung des Fiesco zu Genua*, engraving by Karl Moritz Lämmel.[11]

Schiller takes over the uninhibited display of creative energy, the audaciousness and immorality of Fiesco's actions as well as his independence, his apparent disinterestedness and dissimulation. But the most significant change to the historical facts is with Fiesco's death – whereas the historical Fiesco had fallen accidentally to his death in the harbour of Genoa, in Schiller's play his fellow conspirator Verrina pushes him into the sea. This ending was the result of Schiller treating Fiesco as a tragic character. Fiesco is blind to his faults and fails to heed warnings. He plays with the idea of power in his imagination and feels himself superior to the artist Romano,

---

11 Image from Wikimedia Commons: https://commons.wikimedia.org/wiki/File:Friedrich_Pecht_gez,_Schiller-Galerie,_Friedrich_von_Schiller,_Sammelbild,_Stahlstich_um_1859,_Fiesco_aus_Die_Verschw%C3%B6rung_des_Fiesco_zu_Genua,_Karl_Moritz_L%C3%A4mmel.jpg. Scan by Bernd Schwabe, CC BY 3.0.

who presents to him his tableau depicting the rape of Virgina by Appius Claudius. The painter merely depicts past events, Fiesco claims, whereas he believes he can control them as they are happening. Fiesco's fate follows the pattern of Aristotelian tragedy in which the hero loses contact with reality, overestimates his own powers, leading to his destruction. In addition, many elements of Schiller's play come from Shakespearean tragedy. The idea of basing character tragedy on a historical conspiracy is Shakespearean. There are verbal reminiscences of *Hamlet*, *Macbeth* and *Othello*,[12] and thematic links to *Coriolanus* and *Julius Caesar*. As Caesar is warned of the Ides of March, Fiesco is warned by the Moor to beware of Doria. Fiesco has elements of Caesar (charisma, yet aloofness and the potential to become a tyrant) as well as of the conspirators (deviousness, the underdog, a rebel against tyranny), while Verrina owes something to Shakespeare's Brutus (nobility, and tragically divided). Leonora is Fiesco's Portia, but while Shakespeare's Portia kills herself, Schiller compounds Fiesco's guilt by making him her accidental murderer.

The leaning on Shakespeare shows how in his second play Schiller was learning his trade. His *Fiesco* can be seen as several plays merged into one. It has been called 'a republican play without republicans,' but it is wrong to look for an analysis of republicanism in the modern sense or even from the point of view of Schiller's own time. Although it deals with republicanism as an alternative to tyranny, the reasons for the failure of the rebellion are to be found in the character of Fiesco rather than the political situation. It is a historical drama but not in the sense that, like Schiller's later plays, it attempts to show a pattern in the workings of history such as a triadic scheme which points to a goal in the future. Rather, it attempts to examine the remarkable and mysterious character that is Fiesco. Although he has a legitimate grudge against tyranny in Genoa that will come about by the handing of power from the aged Andrea Doria to his younger, depraved nephew Gianettino, he soon becomes obsessed by the idea of the acquisition of power and greatness. He is playing a part in a play, and so involved is

---

12 How like the words in the anonymous letter to Brutus, 'Speak, strike, redress!' (*Julius Caesar* II, 1) is the artisans' exhortation to Fiesco: 'Strike! Throw down! Set free!' (*Fiesco* II, 8) before he relates to them an allegory of the sharing of power in the animal kingdom so reminiscent of Menenius' belly speech in *Coriolanus*; Verrina's 'When do we meet again?' (*Fiesco* II, 19) to the witches in *Macbeth*; Leonora's 'Let me not pronounce it in your hearing, virginal light!' (*Fiesco* III, 3) to Othello's 'Let me not name it to you, you chaste stars!' (*Othello* V, 2). Schiller read Shakespeare's works in Wieland's prose translations.

he, that he does not sense the potential for events to get out of control. He is unable to achieve the ideal balance between the senses and reason that Schiller believed necessary. He aspires to be great by being seen to do great deeds in the services of what appears to be a political aim. But his egotism gets the better of him. For he knows that politics can be a pretend game and that being seen to be great is a matter of convincing others that you are. He is duped by himself and is his own undoing. He has no real antagonist: neither Andrea Doria, to whom he is opposed but with whom there is no confrontation, nor his former ally Verrina, who sends him to his death. Together they constitute his nemesis.

There are some ways in which Schiller's play does not conform to the pattern of classical tragedy. Not everything emanates from the hero's tragic flaw. The action of the play is carefully motivated and dependent on characters' behaviour, but there is also a sense of random events and the arbitrariness of fate. This makes the play seem modern. Schiller at this stage of his life was interested in chaos, evil and the interdependence of mind and body rather than the power of the mind to influence events and the conformity of events to a pattern. Thus we find Fiesco himself saying: 'What reason, that busy ant, drags together laboriously an accidental gust can heap up in an instant' (Act II, Scene 4). Indeed, the fact that Schiller toyed with different endings is proof that he believed events could take a different turn. The Moor Muley Hassan embodies this unpredictability, and the association with chaos and evil. He pays the price for this and becomes a victim of Fiesco's revenge and a victim of nemesis.

Schiller chose to incorporate into his drama what amounts to two other plays that are essentially domestic tragedies, the form of literary drama that had established itself in Germany when he was beginning to write at the end of the 1770s. The first involves Fiesco's love life. Although he loves his wife Leonora (who is also admired by one of the conspirators, Calcagno), he pursues Julia, the young widowed sister of Gianettino Doria, and then humiliates her in Leonora's presence. Fiesco accidentally murders the faithful Leonora, thinking that she is Gianettino, in whose cloak she has disguised herself. It is the climax to the tragic misadventures of a libertine and sensualist. But it also points to a deeper split in the hero's mind which shows that love, domestic life and politics don't mix. This is made clear in Leonora's eloquent speech in Act IV, Scene 14, in which she weighs up the claims of ambition for power and love. Although she is a sentimental character, she yet reflects Fiesco's weaknesses and her death is a consequence of his excesses. As in his later plays, Schiller reveals what it is like to be a woman in a man's world.

The other domestic tragedy is the plot surrounding the conspirator Verrina's daughter Berta, which owes much to Lessing's reworking of the Virginia story in *Emilia Galotti*. Berta is raped by the brutish Gianettino, cursed by her father and locked away. Unlike Emilia, Berta herself is of little psychological interest, and Schiller focuses on her father's dilemma, integrating the political with the family matter. The play has even been seen (somewhat inflatedly perhaps) as Verrina's tragedy.[13] In this view, domestic tragedy has been moved up a notch to become a matter of state. To be sure, it ends happily, for Berta is reunited with her lover, the noble young conspirator Bourgognino (and true to the form of Shakespearean comedy, she appears in the guise of a young boy). Here, as elsewhere, the play has elements of comedy showing another side to the serious elements, as in the case of Julia Imperiali. There is a comic side to Leonora's character inasmuch as she appears as the typical woman of sensibility led by her emotions.[14] The figure of the Moor, Muley Hassan, also creates levity with his obsequiousness, bluntness, and ostentatiously clipped language. He flatters his master and disguises his own motives. Like one of Shakespeare's fools he makes nonsensical statements like, 'My feet have their hands full' (Act II, Scene 15). He is a character who, although improbable in some respects (Gianettino rather naively puts his trust in him and he rapidly switches allegiances) is linked to the serious themes of the play. He is unlike the Shakespearean fool in that he represents moral evil and Fiesco's failure to see that underscores his tragedy.

Links to other forms of theatre, like the Italian *commedia dell'arte*, in which masks and costume are given priority over realism are striking. *Fiesco* is a play in which masks play a crucial role, especially at the outset and denouement, but with the metaphor of the mask ever present. The play opens with a masked ball that Fiesco has arranged. It enables him to exhibit his virtuosity and skills of control and manipulation. But his wife Leonora tears off her mask in disgust at her husband's philandering. Gianettino Doria wearing a green mask commissions the Moor Muely Hassan to murder Fiesco in a white mask. All the conspirators-to-be are masked, suggesting intrigue and deception rather than full-blooded republican idealism. Moreover, the conspirators are linked to the depravity of their

---

13 Kluge, Commentary to WB 2, pp. 1225-1227.
14 See Nikola Roßbach, *Schiller-Handbuch*, p. 61.

opponents through masks: after the masked ball we are told that Berta has been raped by the masked man in the green coat, the hated Gianettino Doria. All this points to the problems Fiesco will encounter by virtue of his desire to impress, control, manipulate. The revenge of the mask occurs in the final act when Fiesco accidentally murders his wife, who has disguised herself in Gianettino's scarlet cloak. He interprets this as a sign from heaven. Fiesco's nemesis has come. The mask has fallen; he experiences the shame and agony of not having his wife by his side as the newly proclaimed Duke. He has been beaten at his own game.

Beneath the masks, we find not just humans but humans that can behave like animals. Characters constantly refer to one another, sometimes half in jest, as a type of animal. Some of this is proverbial, but the recurrent imagery tells us there is a thin line between man's potential for nobility and his propensity to follow his instinctual nature. The Moor offers himself to Fiesco as 'your tracking hound, your coursing hound, your fox, your snake, your go-between and henchman.' *'One fox can sniff out another,'* Fiesco says to him. Though Fiesco aspires to be the noble lion and rule over all animals, he strikes back like a cornered beast. The animal metaphors resurface on a broader level. 'Is it exactly a pleasure to be the foot of this sluggish many-legged beast of a *republic*,' Fiesco asks. Genoa the Republic becomes a sacrificial animal; Verrina tells Fiesco that he has torn Genoa from Andreas Doria, just as a wolf tears the lamb from its mother. In the Genoese world of politics it is the law of the jungle that prevails. Schiller shows us in *Fiesco* how reason is constantly in danger of being overpowered by man's animal nature.

While elements of both comedy and tragedy can be seen to have been borrowed from various sources, the distinctive feature of Schiller's early plays is their language. Here again, Schiller was influenced by the same models. Thus we sense the power of rhetoric used to sway the people in Menenius's famous belly speech from *Coriolanus* in Fiesco's tale of the lion and the dog with which he addresses the artisans. Time and again we find character's making general statements about human affairs that remind us of characters in Lessing's plays. (One example must suffice: compare Gianettino I, 5, 'Force is the most effective form of persuasion,' with Emilia's words, 'Seduction is true force,' in V, 7 of *Emilia Galotti*.) The Bible was also an important source of inspiration for Schiller's language. At the same time the sources fade into the background and there are many distinctively original marks in Schiller's language. The interlocking dialogue between Verrina and Fiesco in the penultimate scene is a good illustration. Verrina's cross-questioning, one character's repetition of the other's words and phrases, or of their own, thrust and counter-thrust, produce sustained tension and pathos, a climactic ending to the political battle which decides the fate of Genoa.[15] This is heightened by the use of stage directions (e.g. *'very moved.' 'more pressing.' 'with terrible scorn'*). Schiller's use of gesture continues along the path begun by Lessing towards a more expressive dramatic language and goes much further, injected as it is with the emotions of the *Sturm und Drang*: there is an abundance of bodily movement and gesture which emphasises the spontaneity of the action, and is often extreme. Thus the play opens with two characters, Rosa and Arabella rushing onto the stage in disarray, Leonora ripping off her mask and throwing herself into a chair before rising to her feet; it ends with the violence of Fiesco being pushed into the sea.

Nineteenth-century theatre directors in Germany gradually found their way to Schiller's play and it had some notable performances. Although it has not been as frequently performed in Germany as Schiller's other plays, it has held its place on the German stage into the twenty-first century and appears again and again. In the twentieth century, it established itself in the repertoire and made the transition to silent film (in 1921) and television (in 1961 and 1999).

Like other works by Schiller, *Fiesco* was first translated into English during Schiller's lifetime. The play had some great admirers in England (more than one reviewer thought it Schiller's best play) but some detractors too, who criticised improbabilities, characters they found to be repugnant or the play's extreme style and excessive length. The first translation, by G. H. Noehden and J. Stoddart, attempted to tone down Schiller's language.[16] Sir Walter Scott, strongly interested in German 'plays of Chivalry' and thinking that Schiller's Fiesco had not yet been translated into English had, by 1798, undertaken his own translation, but it remained published.[17] There were

---

15 See p. 121. FIESCO. The rotter was putting Genoa to the torch.
VERRINA. But *that* rotter nonetheless spared the laws?
FIESCO. Verrina is torching my friendship.
VERRINA. So much for friendship.
This is a technique which Schiller develops to great effect in his later plays.
16 G. H. Noehden and J. Stoddart, *Fiesco, or the Genoese Conspiracy. A Tragedy Translated from the German of F. Schiller* (London 1796). William Taylor points out that Schiller's line 'Werde du eine *Hure* –' is weakened to: 'And thou may'st become a prey to dishonour!' See William Taylor, review of *Fiesco, Monthly Review*, n.s. 22 (1797), pp. 204-206.
17 See Scott's letter of 5 May 1798 to the pubishers 'Messrs. Cadell & Davies.' Ruth M.

a handful more translations into English in the nineteenth century. One of them, by Colonel d'Aguilar in 1832 is mostly into prose, but sometimes blank verse. There was much praise for it at the time, though it scarcely reproduces the full range of Schiller's language and comes dangerously close to plagiarising Shakespeare.[18] The translator explains in his preface that the weaknesses of the play and its exaggerations, were a direct result of the German language and of 'the German school.'[19] And so he tried to soften the blow, to polish and refine the play for an English audience. A prose translation appeared anonymously in 1841,[20] but surprisingly, the translator makes an exception to prose for Fiesco's monologue in Act III, where he uses blank verse in an attempt to heighten pathos. He also adds a scene, 'Berta in the Dungeon.' which Schiller wrote after the first version of the play and which was inserted at the beginning of Act V for the Mannheim stage version. This translation was followed by the publication in 1849 of a revised version of the first translation by Noehden and Stoddart in the Bohn's Standard Library, which helped to bring Schiller's name into the household, was also published in the United States and carried through into the twentieth century, alongside another translation by Edward Pearson, which appeared in the 1890s.[21]

Schiller's *Fiesco* has rarely been performed in Britain. There was an isolated professional performance at Drury Lane Theatre in 1850, when it was adapted to the 'exigencies of the English stage' by a certain Mr. Planché, with the excision of several scenes and the addition of others.[22] The *Observer* reviewer found much to praise in the production, particularly the evocation of history and locality, but the play he thought to be without 'dramatic ingenuity, female interest, or skilful concatenation of events.'[23]

Adams, 'A Letter by Sir Walter Scott,' in: *University of Rochester Library Bulletin* 11 (1956). https://www.lib.rochester.edu/index.cfm?PAGE=3430

18 *Fiesco, Or The Conspiracy of Fiesco at Genoa. An Historical Tragedy translated from the German of Schiller*. The copy in the Bodleian Library, Oxford shows the translation to be by 'the late Col. George d'Aguilar.' The title page has a quotation from Shakespeare's *Henry VIII* (Act IV, Scene I, ll. 440-442): Cromwell, I charge thee, fling away ambition, / By that sin fell the angels; how can man then, / The image of his maker, hope to win by it?

19 Ibid., p. ii.

20 *Fiesco, the Conspiracy of Genoa; A Tragedy. Translated from the German of Friedrich von Schiller. In Five Acts* (London 1841).

21 Edward Stanhope Pearson, *The Conspiracy of Fiesco at Genoa. A republican tragedy in 5 acts, translated* (Dresden 1896).

22 *The Observer*, February 10 1850, p. 6.

23 Ibid.

Whether the translation used was a factor in this lack of success is an open question but it is not surprising that, given the complexities of its plot and the many scene changes required, *Fiesco* did not find a place on the English stage. Performances in this country have been limited to those by university students of German and by fringe theatres (in English);[24] it has not been part of the renaissance of interest in Schiller's plays that has created such successful productions in the West End and regional theatres in recent decades.[25]

There was not only a need for a new translation of Schiller's play for the twenty-first century, but for a full and accurate translation altogether. Unlike some of the earlier translations, which used a hybrid text, the translation offered here is based on the first version of the play, which Schiller published in book form and which, as we have suggested, can be considered the most authentic and original version of the play.[26] The language of Schiller's early plays is often extreme, with some difficult metaphors. But it is also often immensely powerful. Flora Kimmich's translation achieves, in the first instance, accuracy and completeness. There is no attempt to tone down Schiller's language, make it more poetic, less compressed, or to eradicate obscurities. Her translation conveys the energy, intensity and roughness, the occasional elaborateness that Schiller's prose drama abounds in. It gives us the full flavour of the original without overly attempting to update or modify it. It has the faithfulness a good translation requires. At the same it does not attempt to archaise and use a form dramatic dialogue in English that might have been a parallel to that of Schiller's. It is a long overdue translation of Schiller's play as well as one for the twenty-first century.

---

24 A production in German at Balliol College, Oxford in 1983. A highly successful production by the Faction Theatre Company, dir. Mark Leipacher, was staged at the New Diorama Theatre in London in 2013. Nevertheless, the reviewer of the Faction production was also critical of the 'intentional anachronisms' and modernisation of the translation. See Roger Smith, *One-Stop Arts.com*, 10th January 2013. The text used, *Schiller's Fiesco* by Daniel Millar and Mark Leipacher (unpublished), is a substantially condensed version and thus an adaptation rather than a translation.

25 See John Guthrie, 'Classical German Drama on the British Stage. Schiller's *Wallenstein* at the Chichester Festival,' *Modern Drama* 54 (2011), 121-140.

26 The text can be found in volume 4 of the Nationalausgabe and volume 2 of the Frankfurter Ausgabe of Schiller's works.

THE CONSPIRACY OF FIESCO AT GENOA

A Republican Tragedy

> Nam id facinus inprimis ego memorabile existimo
> sceleris atque periculi novitate.
> Sallust, said of Catiline[1]

Dedicated
to Professor Abel
of Stuttgart.

I have drawn the history of the conspiracy primarily from Cardinal Retz's[2] *Conjuration du Comte Jean Louis de Fièsque,* from *L'Histoire des Conjurations, L'Histoire de Gênes,* and from Robertson's[3] *History of Charles V,* part 3. The Hamburg dramaturg[4] will forgive me the liberties I have taken with events if these liberties have succeeded. If they have not, I would rather have spoiled *my* fantasies than the facts. The actual catastrophe of the complot, where the Count is undone by unhappy chance just as he realizes his desires, necessarily had to be changed, for drama, by its very nature, can tolerate neither a random event nor the direct intervention of Providence. I would wonder why no tragic poet has ever worked with this material, did I not find sufficient grounds in just this undramatic turn of events. Higher spirits see the fragile spider webs of a deed run through the entire space of the universe and perhaps attach themselves to the remotest boundaries of the future and the past, while man sees only the free-floating fact. But the artist elects the short view of humanity, whom he wants to instruct, not sharp-sighted omnipotence, from which he learns.

In my *Robbers*[5] I took as my subject the victim of an excessive sensibility. Here I attempt the opposite: a victim of artifice and cabal. Yet, however notable Fiesco's ill-fated project became in history, it can just as easily fail of this effect on the stage. If it is true that only feeling stirs feeling, then, it seems to me, the *political hero* would be no subject for the stage to the extent that he must subordinate his human self in order to be a political hero. It was therefore not my task to breathe into my story the living fire that prevails in a pure product of enthusiasm, but rather to spin a cold, sterile political drama from the materials of the human heart and in just this way to reattach it to the human heart--to compose the *man* from his *politically canny intellect*--and to gather from an inventive intrigue situations for all humanity: *that* was my task. My relations with a bourgeois world have also made me better acquainted with the heart than with the privy council, and perhaps just this political weakness has become a poetical strength.

Dramatis personae[6]

1. ANDREA DORIA, DOGE OF GENOA.[7]
   Honourable elder, eighty years of age. Traces of fieriness. A principal characteristic: weightiness and rigorous, commanding terseness.

2. GIANETTINO DORIA. ANDREA'S NEPHEW.[8] PRETENDER.
   Twenty-six-year-old man. Coarse and offensive in speech, gait, and manners. A peasant's pride. Physically repellent.
   Both Dorias wear scarlet.

3. FIESCO, COUNT OF LAVAGNA.[9] HEAD OF THE CONSPIRACY.
   Slender, very handsome young man of twenty-three. Proud but dignified, friendly yet majestic, courtly and accommodating, and thus cunning.
   All noblemen wear black. The costume is consistently old German style.[10]

4. VERRINA. REPUBLICAN CONSPIRATOR.
   Sixty-year-old man. Ponderous, grave, and somber. Deeply marked.

5. BOURGOGNINO. CONSPIRATOR.
   Twenty-year-old youth. Noble and attractive. Proud, impulsive, and natural.

6. CALCAGNO. CONSPIRATOR.
   Gaunt voluptuary. Thirty years old. Pleasant, enterprising appearance.

7. SACCO. CONSPIRATOR.
   Forty-five-year-old man. Ordinary human being.

8. LOMELLINO. GIANETTINO'S CONFIDANT.
   Hardened courtier.

9. CENTURIONE.

10. CIBO. MALCONTENTS.

11. ASSERATO.

12. ROMANO. PAINTER.
    Unconstrained, candid, and proud.

13. MULEY HASSAN. MOOR FROM TUNIS.[11]
   Convicted Moorish type. In physiognomy an original mixture of knavery and caprice.

14. GERMAN SOLDIERS OF THE DUCAL BODYGUARD.
   Honest simplicity. Reliable bravery.

15. THREE REBELLIOUS CITIZENS.

16. LEONORA. FIESCO'S WIFE.[12]
   Eighteen-year-old noblewoman. Pale and thin. Fragile and sensitive. Very attractive but not dazzling. Her face expresses fantasizing melancholy. Dressed in black.

17. JULIA, DOWAGER COUNTESS IMPERIALI. DORIA'S SISTER.
   Twenty-five-year-old noblewoman. Tall and ample. Proud coquette. Her beauty spoiled by bizarre touches. Dazzling but not pleasing. Her face expresses an unkind, mocking nature. Dressed in black.

18. BERTA. VERRINA'S DAUGHTER.
   Innocent girl.

19. ROSA.

20. ARABELLA. LEONORA'S CHAMBERMAIDS.

NOBLEMEN. CITIZENS. GERMAN BODYGUARDS. SOLDIERS. SERVANTS. THIEVES.

THE PLACE IS GENOA, THE TIME 1547.

Act One

A hall in Fiesco's palace. Dance music is heard in the distance and the tumult of a ball.

Scene 1

Leonora, masked. Rosa and Arabella rush onto the stage in disarray.

LEONORA (*ripping off her mask*). No more! Not another word! Now we know. (*Throws herself into a chair.*) This is too much for me.

ARABELLA. My Lady--

LEONORA (*rising to her feet*). Before my very eyes! A notorious coquette! In plain view of the entire Genoese nobility. (*Sadly.*) Rosa! Bella! And before my eyes, my weeping eyes.

ROSA. Take it for what it really was--a bit of gallantry--

LEONORA. Gallantry? --And their eager exchange of glances? His anxious watching for her next move? That long kiss on her bare arm that left the print of his teeth, bright red? Ha! And the way he sank into a deep, motionless reverie, the *very picture of delight*, as if the world had vanished around him and he were *alone with this* Julia, in eternal nothingness? Gallantry? You sweet child who've never loved, don't tell *me* about love and gallantry.

ROSA. So much the better, Madonna! Lose one husband, gain ten cavaliers.

LEONORA. Lose? --One skipped heartbeat of feeling and I've lost Fiesco? Out of my sight, you wicked chatterbox. --A bit of innocent teasing--perhaps a bit of gallantry. Isn't it so, my sensitive Bella?

ARABELLA. Oh, yes! Exactly right!

LEONORA (*lost in thought*). Would she know she has his *heart* just for that? --Would *her* name lie concealed behind his every thought? --Speak to him in every trace of Nature? --What is this? Where is this leading? Would the world, in all its majesty and beauty, be for him nothing but a magnificent diamond in which *her image--her image* alone--is engraved?

--Would he be in love with her? --With Julia? Oh, give me your arm--steady me, Bella!

(Pause. Music is heard again.)

LEONORA *(starting out of her reverie)*. Listen! Wasn't that Fiesco's voice, over all the noise? Can he laugh when his Leonora is alone and weeping? But no, my child. It was Gianettino Doria, his peasant's voice.

ARABELLA. That's what it was, Signora. But come into another room.

LEONORA. Why so pale, Bella? You're lying-- I can see it in your eyes--and in the faces of the Genoese--something, something. *(Covering her face.)* Oh, for sure, these Genoese know more than a wife is permitted to hear.

ROSA. Oh, jealousy, jealousy! How it exaggerates everything!

LEONORA *(melancholy, rapt)*. When he was still Fiesco, came toward us in the orange grove, where we girls were out walking, Apollo in the bloom of youth, melted into manly, beautiful Antinous--[13] Proud and lordly as he approached us, as if all *ducal Genoa* rested on his young shoulders. Our eyes stole after him and then shied back, as if caught robbing a church, when they met his flashing gaze. Ah, Bella, how we fed upon his glances. How enviously we all feared that they were meant for the next girl. They fell among us like Paris's golden apple: smiling eyes turned more fiery, a peaceful breast turned more stormy, jealousy had divided us.

ARABELLA. I remember. All womankind, every Genoese mother and daughter, was in uproar over this fine conquest.

LEONORA *(in rapture)*. And then to call him *my own*! Daring, terrible good fortune! Genoa's greatest man, *all mine (with poise)*, who sprang perfected from the chisel of the ever-fruitful sculptress, who combined in loveliest nuance all the great men of his noble house. --Listen, girls. Since I can no longer keep it secret. --Listen. I'll confide something, *(confidentially)* a thought that came to me--as I stood at Fiesco's side before the altar--his hand in mine. I had the thought that a *wife* is *forbidden* to think: Fiesco, whose hand now rests in yours--your Fiesco--softly, now! Let no man overhear us, how we are making bold with mere crumbs of his excellence--this Fiesco, your Fiesco--woe betide you, if this doesn't lift your feelings--*will--deliver our Genoa from its tyrants*!

ARABELLA (*amazed*). And this thought occurred to a woman on her wedding day?

LEONORA. Amazing, isn't it? To the bride in the joy of her wedding day. (*More lively*.) I may be a woman-- But I feel the nobility of my descent. I cannot endure how this house of *Doria* wants to tower over our own ancestors. Sweet-tempered Andrea--it is a delight to love him--let him be Duke of Genoa forever. But Gianettino is his nephew--his heir--and Gianettino has an insolent, arrogant heart. Genoa trembles before him, and Fiesco (*falling into melancholy*), Fiesco--weep for me--Fiesco is in love with his sister.

ARABELLA. Poor, unhappy Lady--

LEONORA. And now just go and have a look at this demigod of the Genoese, sitting in the shameless company of revellers and easy women, tickling their ears with rude jokes, spinning tales of enchanted princesses-- That is Fiesco! --Oh, girls, Genoa didn't just lose its hero-- I have lost my husband!

ROSA. Speak more softly. Someone's coming through the gallery.

LEONORA (*starting*). Fiesco's coming.[14] Run! Run! The sight of me could give him a bad moment. (*She leaps into the next room. Her maids follow her.*)

Scene 2

Gianettino Doria, masked, in a green cloak. A Moor. The two in conversation.

GIANETTINO. You have understood.

MOOR. Very well.

GIANETTINO. The white mask.

MOOR. Very well.

GIANETTINO. I repeat--the white mask.

MOOR. Very well! Very well! Very well!

GIANETTINO. You understand? If you miss, it hits *here* (*pointing to his own breast*).

MOOR. No need to worry.

GIANETTINO. And a good, hard thrust!

MOOR. My Lord will be content.

GIANETTINO (*gloating*). Let the poor Count not suffer long.

MOOR. By your leave--about how heavy would his head weigh in the scale?

GIANETTINO. One hundred sequins[15] heavy.

MOOR (*blows on his palm*). Pooh! Light as a feather.

GIANETTINO. What are you muttering?

MOOR. I said--light work.

GIANETTINO. That is your concern. This man is a magnet. He attracts all the troublemakers. Look, you: Do this thing right.

MOOR. But, Master-- I'll have to escape to Venice right after it's done.

GIANETTINO. Then take your reward in advance. (*Tosses him a bill.*) In three days, at the latest. (*Exit.*)

MOOR (*picking up the bill*). Now that's credit. My Lord trusts a rascal's word without a warranty. (*Exit.*)

Scene 3

Calcagno, followed by Sacco. Both in black cloaks.

CALCAGNO. I notice you're watching my every movement.

SACCO. And I observe that you're hiding them all from me. Listen, Calcagno, for some weeks now your face shows something at work in you that doesn't exactly have to do with our fatherland. I would think that we, being brothers, could trade one secret for another and lose nothing in the bargain. --Will you be forthright?

CALCAGNO. So much so that my heart will meet you halfway on my tongue, if you don't want to plumb my breast. --I'm in love with the Countess Fiesco.

SACCO (*steps back in wonderment*). *That* I never would have figured out, even if I had considered every possibility. --Your choice stretches my wit on the rack and will break it if you meet with success.

CALCAGNO. They say she is an example of strictest virtue.

SACCO. They're lying. She is the full article, not a dog-eared excerpt. One or the other, Calcagno: either give up this pursuit or take your heart out of it--

CALCAGNO. The Count is unfaithful to her. Jealousy is the sliest matchmaker. An attempt against the Dorias would keep the Count busy and give me things to do at the palace. While he is chasing the wolf away from the flock, the marten will get into his henhouse.

SACCO. You're incorrigible, brother. And thanks. You've cured me, too, of blushing. What I was ashamed to think I can now say out loud: I'm reduced to begging, if the present constitution doesn't get thrown out.

CALCAGNO. Are you that deep in debt?

SACCO. So deep that my lifeline, four times doubled, would snap on the first tenth of it. A new government will give me breathing room, I hope. Even if it doesn't help me *pay*, it should spoil my creditors' appetite for making *demand*.

CALCAGNO. I see. --And, in the end, if Genoa frees itself *at this opportunity*, Sacco will consent to being called a Father of the Fatherland.[16] Well, tell me again that old tale about probity, now that the bankruptcy of a wastrel and the lust of a wanton determine the fortunes of the State! By God, Sacco! I admire Heaven's fine speculation in us: using the leaking boils on the body's limbs to save its heart. --Does Verrina know of your plot?

SACCO. As much as that patriot should know. *Genoa*, you too know, is the spindle around which all his thoughts turn, with steely loyalty. He now has his eagle eye on Fiesco. He hopes that you, too, are halfway inclined toward a bold plot.

CALCAGNO. He has a fine nose. Come, let's go seek him out and fan his feelings for freedom with our own. (*Exeunt*.)

Scene 4

Julia, excited. Fiesco, in a white cloak, hurries after her.

JULIA. Lackeys! Runners!

FIESCO. Countess, where are you going? What are you thinking?

JULIA. Nothing, nothing at all. (*Servants*.) My carriage to the door!

FIESCO. By your leave--no. There has been some offense.

JULIA. Pooh! Hardly. --Let me go! You're tearing my ruffle to pieces. --Offense? Who is there here who can give offense? Please go away.

FIESCO (*on one knee*). Not before you tell me who has been so bold--

JULIA (*stands still, hands on hips*). Oh, excellent, excellent. A sight to see. We ought to summon the Countess Lavagna to this charming spectacle. --Tell me, Count, is this the faithful husband? This pose belongs in your wife's bedchamber, when she is checking her record of caresses and they will not add up. Stand up, I tell you. And betake yourself to ladies who'll give you a better bargain. Stand up! Or are you offering your gallantries as penance for your wife's impertinences?

FIESCO (*leaps up*). Impertinent? Toward you?

JULIA. To take her departure--push back her chair--turn her back to the table--the table, Count, where *I* am seated.

FIESCO. Unpardonable.

JULIA. Nothing *more* than that? --What a farce! And is it my fault (*smiling to herself*) that the Count has eyes?

FIESCO. It is the fault of your beauty, Madonna, that he doesn't have eyes for everyone.

JULIA. No fine speeches, Count, when honour is the subject. I demand satisfaction. Shall I find it with you? Or in the Duke's thunderous response?

FIESCO. In the arms of love, which begs pardon for a faux pas born of jealousy.

JULIA. Jealousy? Jealousy? What does that little dunce want? (*Gesticulating before a mirror.*) Can she find any better testimonial to her taste than that I declare it for my own? (*Proudly.*) Doria and Fiesco? --Must the Countess Lavagna not feel honoured that the Duke's niece finds her choice enviable? (*Amicably, offering her hand to be kissed.*) If we suppose that I do find it so.

FIESCO (*vividly*). Atrocious, my Lady. --And still you go on torturing me! --I well know, divine Julia, that I should feel only respect for you. Reason tells me to bend my subject's knee before the house of Doria. But my heart worships the lovely Julia. My love is an outlaw, but also a hero, bold enough to breach the city walls of rank and to soar up toward the consuming sun of majesty.

JULIA. A great, great lordly lie that lurches along on stilts. --His Lordship's tongue tells me that I am god-like, and yet his leaping heart lies under the silhouette[17] of another.

FIESCO. Or rather, Signora, my heart beats against it unwillingly and wants to push it away. (*Removing Leonora's silhouette, on a sky-blue ribbon, and giving it to Julia.*) Erect *your* image on this altar, and you can destroy this false god.

JULIA (*takes the locket quickly; with satisfaction*). A great sacrifice, by my honour, deserving of my thanks. (*She hangs her image around his neck.*) There, slave, wear the colours of thy master. (*Exit.*)

FIESCO (*ardently*). Julia loves me. Julia! I envy no god. (*Pacing joyfully.*) Let this night be a festival of the gods, a masterpiece of joy. Holla! Holla! (*Many Servants.*) Rivers of Cyprian wine through my halls, music to wake midnight from its leaden slumber, a thousand burning lamps to mock the morning sun! --Let there be pleasure everywhere, bacchantic dancing to stamp the realm of the dead to pieces! (*He hurries away. Noisy allegro as* a scrim is raised to reveal a large, brightly lit ballroom where many Masks are dancing. On the sides, Guests at gambling tables and tables offering wine.)

Scene 5

Gianettino, half-drunk. Lomellino. Cibo. Centurione. Verrina. Sacco. Calcagno. All masked. A number of ladies and gentlemen of the Nobility.

GIANETTINO (*noisily*). Bravo! Bravo! These wines go down famously, our lovely dancers leap à merveille. One of you go spread the word in Genoa that I am in fine spirits; they should regale themselves. --A red-letter day, as sure as I live. Put it in the calendar: Today Prince Doria made merry.

GUESTS (*lift their glasses*). The Republic! (*Trumpet blast.*)

GIANETTINO (*hurls his glass to the floor*). Smashed to pieces. (*Three black Masks spring up, gather around Gianettino.*)

LOMELLINO (*brings the Prince forward*). My Lord, you mentioned to me lately a young person whom you had seen at San Lorenzo?[18]

GIANETTINO. That I did, fellow, and want to make her acquaintance.

LOMELLINO. I can arrange it for Your Grace.

GIANETTINO (*quickly*). Can you? Can you indeed? --Lomellino, you put your name on the list for the office of Procurator[19] lately. You shall have it.

LOMELLINO. My Gracious Prince, it is the second-highest office in the land. More than sixty noblemen are contending for it, all richer and more respected than Your Grace's humble servant.

GIANETTINO (*snorting aggressively*). Damnation and Doria. You shall be Procurator. (*The three Masks come forward.*) Genoese noblemen? Let them toss all their ancestors and all their coats of arms into the scale at once: add one hair from the hoary beard of my uncle, and the whole Genoese nobility is outweighed. I so *desire*, and you *shall* be Procurator. That amounts to all the votes of the Signoria.[20]

LOMELLINO (*softly*). The girl is the only daughter of a certain Verrina.

GIANETTINO. The girl is pretty and, by God, I'll have her.

LOMELLINO. My Gracious Lord, the only child of the most obstinate Republican!

GIANETTINO. The devil take your Republican! The anger of a vassal and my desire! You're saying the Lanterna[21] must collapse when boys toss seashells at it. (*The three Masks close in, gesturing broadly.*) Did Duke Andrea collect his scars in the battles of these rag-tag Republicans so that his nephew would have to seek the favours of their daughters and their brides on bended knee? Damnation and Doria! They'll have to swallow my demand, or over the bones of my uncle I'll erect a gallows and their Genoese freedom will swing from it. (*The three Masks step back.*)

LOMELLINO. The girl is *alone* just now. Her father is present *here*. He's one of the three masks.

GIANETTINO. Perfect, Lomellino. Bring me to her right away.

LOMELLINO. But you'll be expecting a courtesan, and you'll find a *bundle of feelings*.

GIANETTINO. Force is the most effective form of persuasion. Bring me to her instantly. I'd like to see the republican dog that leaps up on the Dorian bear. (*Bumps into Fiesco in the doorway.*) Where is the Countess?

Scene 6

As above, Fiesco.

FIESCO. I have handed her into her carriage. (*Seizes Gianettino's hand and holds it against his breast.*) Prince, now I am doubly bound to you. Gianettino rules over my head and over Genoa, and your delightful sister over my heart.

LOMELLINO. Fiesco has become quite an Epicurean. You are a great loss to the world of affairs.

FIESCO. But the world of affairs is no loss to me. To *live* is to *dream*; to be wise, Lomellino, is to *dream good dreams*. Is this better done before a thundering throne, where the turning wheels of state grate eternally upon the ear, than on the breast of a panting woman? Let Gianettino Doria rule over Genoa. Fiesco gives himself to love.

GIANETTINO. Time to go, Lomellino. It's almost midnight. It's time, I say. We're grateful for your hospitality, Lavagna. I was content.

FIESCO. That, Prince, is all that I desire.

GIANETTINO. Good night, then. There's gaming at the palace tomorrow and Fiesco is invited. Come, Procurator.

FIESCO. Music! Lights!

GIANETTINO (*defiantly opening a path through the three Masks*). Make way in the name of the Duke.

ONE OF THE THREE MASKS (*mutters resentfully*). Only in Hell. Never in Genoa.

GUESTS (*moving out*). The Prince is leaving. Good night, Lavagna. (*They stagger out.*)

Scene 7

The three black Masks. Fiesco.
Pause.

FIESCO. I notice guests here who take no part in the pleasures of my evening.

MASKS (*muttering ill-temperedly among themselves*). Oh, surely not.

FIESCO (*obliging*). Should my goodwill send a *single* Genoese away discontented? Quick, lackeys! Refreshments here! Fill the great wine bowls. I wouldn't want anyone to suffer boredom in my halls. May I entertain your eyes with fireworks? Would you like to hear my Harlequin's arts? Perhaps you'll find the ladies of my house diverting? Or shall we sit down to faro and beguile the time with gambling?

A MASK. It is our custom to *purchase* our time with *deeds*.

FIESCO. A manly answer and--this is Verrina!

Act One 17

VERRINA (*removes his mask*). Fiesco discovers his friends in their masks more quickly than they discover him in his.

FIESCO. I don't understand. But what's the meaning of this black mourning band? Can Verrina have lost someone and Fiesco know nothing about it?

VERRINA. A death announcement has no place at Fiesco's festive evenings.

FIESCO. Not so, when a friend calls upon him. (*Presses his hand with warmth.*) Friend of my soul, who is it whom *we've both* lost?

VERRINA. Both! Both! All too true! --But not all sons mourn their mother.

FIESCO. Your mother is long in the grave.

VERRINA (*with meaning*). I recall that Fiesco used to call me brother because I was the son of his fatherland.

FIESCO (*amused*). Oh, is that it? It was all a joke? Mourning garb for Genoa. True enough, Genoa is now on its deathbed. That's a new one. Our cousin is becoming a wit.

CALCAGNO. He means it seriously, Fiesco.

FIESCO. No doubt! No doubt! That's just it. So straight-faced and so lachrymose. A joke loses everything if it's told with a laugh. A face like a pallbearer! I would never have thought that our somber Verrina would become such a wag in his old age.

SACCO. Come, Verrina. He's no longer one of ours.

FIESCO. But merrily, merrily, my fellow countryman. Let's look like the wily heirs who follow the coffin weeping loudly, the better to laugh into their handkerchiefs. Though we may get a wicked stepmother for our pains. No matter! We'll let her rage while we go banqueting.

VERRINA (*very aroused*). In heaven's name! And do nothing? --What has become of you, Fiesco? Where do I find the great tyrant-hater? There was a time when you would have doubled over at the sight of a crown. --You fallen son of the Republic, you will answer for it that I care not one fig for my own immortality, having seen that passing time can wear away the spirit, too.

FIESCO. Always moping. Let him put Genoa in his pocket and peddle it to a pirate from Tunis, what do we care? We'll drink Cyprian wine and kiss the pretty girls.

VERRINA (*observing him gravely*). Is that your real, your honest opinion?

FIESCO. Why not, old friend? Is it exactly a pleasure to be the foot of this sluggish many-legged beast of a *republic*? Thank the one who gives it wings and puts the feet out of service. Gianettino Doria is going to be Duke. Affairs of state will no longer turn us grey.

VERRINA. Fiesco? --Is that your real, your honest opinion?

FIESCO. Andrea is going to declare his nephew his son and make him heir to all his estates. Who would be so foolish as to contest his bequeathing him his power as well?

VERRINA (*deeply displeased*). Come then, men of Genoa. (*He leaves Fiesco abruptly. The others follow.*)

FIESCO. Verrina! --Verrina! --That old Republican is as rigid as steel!

Scene 8

Fiesco. An unknown Mask.

MASK. Do you have a moment, Lavagna?

FIESCO (*graciously*). An hour, if you like.

MASK. Then you would be so good as to accompany me outside the walls?

FIESCO. We're within ten minutes of midnight.

MASK. You would be so good, Count.

FIESCO. I'll order the carriage.

MASK. No need. I'll have a horse sent ahead. No more is needed. Only one of us will re-enter, I hope.

FIESCO (*startled*). And?

MASK. You'll have to answer in blood for certain tears.

FIESCO. And these tears?

MASK. Of a certain Countess Lavagna. I know the lady well and wish to know how she has deserved to be sacrificed to a fool.

FIESCO. Now I understand you. And may I know the name of this curious challenger?

MASK. The very man who once worshipped Cibo's noble daughter[22] and renounced in favour of the bridegroom Fiesco.

FIESCO. Scipio Bourgognino!

BOURGOGNINO (*removing his mask*). And has now come to redeem his honour for yielding to a rival small-minded enough to torment one so sweet-tempered.

FIESCO (*embraces him warmly*). You noble young man. It is thanks to the sorrows of my wife that I make so valuable an acquaintanceship. I appreciate the beauty of your sentiment, but I will not fight.

BOURGOGNINO (*taking a step backward*). Count Lavagna would be too cowardly to risk himself against the first efforts of my sword?

FIESCO. Bourgognino! Against all the might of France, but not against you! I honour this endearing ardour in behalf of an object yet dearer. That spirit deserves a laurel wreath, but the deed would be too childish.

BOURGOGNINO (*excited*). Childish, Count? --Womankind, mistreated, can *only weep*. --What is the man there for?

FIESCO. Uncommonly well said, but I will not fight.

BOURGOGNINO (*turns his back, about to leave*). Then I shall despise you.

FIESCO (*animated*). That, youngster, you shall never do, by God, and if virtue should fall in the market. (*Cautiously takes his hand.*) Have you never felt toward me what one might--how to put it--might call *respect*?

BOURGOGNINO. Would I have renounced in favour of one whom I thought less than first among men?

FIESCO. Very good, my young friend. And I in your place would be slow to feel contempt--for a man who had once deserved my respect. For

I should think that the web of a master weaver would be too artful to be discerned by the fleeting glance of a beginner. --Go home now, Bourgognino, and take the time to *ponder* why Fiesco is proceeding *this* way and not otherwise. (*Bourgognino leaves without speaking.*) Farewell, noble youngster. When these flames leap over onto the *fatherland*, let the house of *Doria* look to its walls.

Scene 9

Fiesco. The Moor enters cautiously and looks around narrowly.

FIESCO (*eyeing him sharply and steadily*). Who are you and what do you want?

MOOR (*as above*). A slave of the Republic.

FIESCO. Slavery is a miserable business. (*Still eyeing him sharply.*) What are you looking for?

MOOR. My Lord, I am an honourable man.

FIESCO. Hang that sign around your neck. It will never be superfluous. --But what are you looking for?

MOOR (*tries to come closer; Fiesco evades*). My Lord, I'm no rogue.

FIESCO. Good that you say so--but also not good. (*Impatient.*) What are you looking for?

MOOR (*coming nearer again*). Are you Count Lavagna?

FIESCO (*proudly*). The blind men of Genoa know me by my tread. --What's the Count to you?

MOOR. Watch out, Lavagna! (*Hard by him.*)

FIESCO (*leaps away*). That I do.

MOOR (*as above*). They don't mean you any good, Lavagna.

FIESCO (*draws back again*). I notice.

MOOR. Watch out for Doria.

FIESCO (*approaches him, more at ease*). Have I done you an injustice, friend? That name I have reason to fear.

MOOR. Then flee from the man. Can you read?

FIESCO. An amusing question. You've had traffic with many a nobleman. Do you have something in writing?

MOOR. Your name among the condemned. (*Hands him a sheet of paper and leans in on him. Fiesco steps in front of a mirror and bends over the sheet. The Moor circles him, choosing his moment, finally draws a dagger and is about to strike.*)

FIESCO (*pivots adroitly and blocks the Moor's arm*). Easy, easy, you dog. (*Seizes the dagger.*)

MOOR (*stamps wildly*). The devil! --Beg pardon. (*Tries to slip away.*)

FIESCO (*seizes him, shouts*). Stefano! Drullo! Antonio! (*Catching the Moor in a chokehold.*) Stay, my good friend. A hellish bit of mischief. (*Servants.*) Stand still and answer me. You've made a bad job of it. Who's paying you?

MOOR (*after many attempts to slip away; firmly*). They can't hang me any higher than the gallows.

FIESCO. No! Console yourself! Not on the horns of the moon, yet high enough still for you to take the gallows for a toothpick. But you chose too diplomatically for this to have been *your* work. Now tell me: Who hired you?

MOOR. My Lord, you may curse me for a villain, but I'll not be called stupid.

FIESCO. Is this beast proud! Speak, you beast, who hired you?

MOOR (*reflecting*). Hm! So maybe I'm not the only fool? --Who hired me? --And for one hundred miserable sequins. --Who hired me? --Prince Gianettino.

FIESCO (*pacing; bitterly*). One hundred sequins and no more? For Fiesco's head? (*Sneering.*) Shame on you, Crown Prince of Genoa. (*Going to a casket.*) Here, fellow, is one thousand, and go tell your master--he's a tight-fisted murderer.

>   (*Moor looks him up and down.*)

FIESCO. You're thinking it over, fellow?

>   (*Moor takes the money, puts it down, picks it up again, looks at him with growing amazement.*)

FIESCO. What are you up to, fellow?

MOOR (*decides and throws the money on the table*). Master--I haven't deserved this money.

FIESCO. The gallows is what you deserve, you thieving dunce. An angry elephant tramples men, but not vermin. I'd have you hanged, if it cost me just two words more.

MOOR (*with a bow; pleased*). My Lord is much too kind.

FIESCO. God forbid. Not toward *you*! It merely pleases me to think that my caprice can make a rogue like you into something or nothing, and that's why you go free. Understand me rightly. Your clumsiness is Heaven's pledge that I've been saved for something great. That's why I've been merciful and you go free.

MOOR (*extending his hand*). Put 'er there, Lavagna. One good turn deserves another. If there's a throat too many for you on this peninsula,[23] only say so, and I'll slit it for you, *for free*.

FIESCO. There's a well-mannered beast. Wants to say its thanks with the throats of strangers.

MOOR. We don't accept gifts, Master. Our kind also has its honour.

FIESCO. The honour of cutthroats?

MOOR. Holds up better than that of your honourable men. *They* break their vows before God Almighty; *we* scrupulously keep ours with the Devil.

FIESCO. You're a droll rascal.

MOOR. Pleased to see you've developed a taste for me. Put me to the test: you'll find a man who can recite his lesson on the spot. Just ask me. I can give you a testimonial on every society of rascals, from the lowest to the highest.

FIESCO. You don't say. (*Seating himself.*) So even scoundrels recognize rules and ranks. Tell me about the lowest one.

MOOR. Pooh, my Lord. That is the despicable army of the *long-fingered*. A wretched trade that never turns out a worthwhile man. Works its way toward the bullwhip or the stone quarry and ends up--at best on the gallows.

FIESCO. A charming end. I'm curious to know the next better.

MOOR. That's the *spies* and *machinators*. Gentlemen of importance to whom the grandees lend an ear, where they get their superior knowledge. They fasten onto souls like leeches, draw off all the venom from the heart, and spew it out again for the *authorities*.

FIESCO. I'm acquainted with that. --Next?

MOOR. Now comes the rank of the assassins, poisoners, and all who track their man and then attack from ambush. Little cowards, often, but still a good sort who pay the Devil's tuition with their wretched souls. Here justice goes one better: straps their joints to the wheel and plants their little noggins on pikes. That's the third society.

FIESCO. But, tell me, when do we get to yours?

MOOR. Ho, ho, my Lord. That's just it: I've made my way through all of them. My genius vaulted early across every preserve. I performed my masterpiece in the third one yesterday, and an hour ago--I botched the fourth.

FIESCO. Which consists of--?

MOOR (*eagerly*). These are the ones (*excited*) who seek out their man within four walls, hack a path for themselves through danger, attack him straight away, and with the first Hello! spare him his thanks for a second one. Between us: They call them the special delivery of Hell. When Mephistopheles feels a craving, it only takes a nod, and he gets the roast still warm from the oven.

FIESCO. You are a sinner from Hell's own kitchen. I've needed such a one for a long time. Give me your hand. I'm going to keep you in my service.

MOOR. Serious or joking?

FIESCO. I'm perfectly serious, and I'll give you one thousand sequins a year.

MOOR. Done, Lavagna! I am all yours and the devil take private life. Use me for what you will. As your tracking hound, your coursing hound, your fox, your snake, your go-between and henchman. For all commissions, Master, but no honest ones--there I'm a dunderhead.

FIESCO. Not to worry. I want to give someone a *lamb*, I'll not send it by way of a *wolf*. Go through all Genoa early tomorrow and catch the scent of things. Find out what they think of the government and what they're whispering about the house of Doria. While you're at it, inquire what my fellow citizens think of my high living and my great romance. Soak their brains in wine until their deepest opinions are flushed out. Here's money. Distribute it among the silk merchants--

MOOR (*looks at him with misgiving*). Master--

FIESCO. Never fear. It's nothing honest. Go now. Call on your whole band for help. I'll hear your news tomorrow. (*Exit.*)

MOOR (*calling after him*). You can count on me. It's four in the morning now. By tomorrow at eight you'll have heard news to fill twice seventy ears.[24] (*Exit.*)

Scene 10

Room in Verrina's house. Berta prostrate on a sofa, holding her head. Verrina enters in a dark mood.

BERTA (*jumps up, startled*). Dear heaven! There he is.

VERRINA (*stops; regards her, surprised*). My daughter is startled at her father's entrance?

BERTA. Oh, flee! Or let me flee! You're terrible, Father.

VERRINA. To my only child?

BERTA (*looks at him, troubled*). Not so. You must have another daughter.

VERRINA. Does my affection oppress you so?

BERTA. It crushes me, Father.

VERRINA. What a reception, Daughter! Earlier, when I came home, weighed down, my Berta would come running and laugh away my cares. Come, Daughter, embrace me. Let your radiance warm my heart, which is turning to ice at the deathbed of my country. Ah, my child, I settled accounts with all the pleasures of Nature today, and (*very heavily*) you alone remain.

BERTA (*appraises him with a long gaze*). Oh, my unhappy father.

VERRINA (*embraces her, depressed*). Berta! My only child! Berta! My last remaining hope! Genoa's freedom--it's finished. --Fiesco, finished. (*Pressing her close, through his teeth.*) Just you become a whore--

BERTA (*tears herself away*). Dear God! You know--?

VERRINA (*rooted to the spot*). What?

BERTA. My honour, my virgin honour--

VERRINA (*in a rage*). What?

BERTA. Last night--

VERRINA (*like a madman*). What?

BERTA. By force! (*She sinks onto the sofa.*)

VERRINA (*after a terrible pause, in a choked voice*). Take just one breath more, Daughter-- Your last. (*His voice hollow, broken.*) Who?

BERTA. Oh, horrible! This bloodless anger! God have mercy! He stammers, he's trembling!

VERRINA. But I wouldn't know-- Daughter! Who?

BERTA. Be calm, be calm, my own, my own precious father.

VERRINA. In God's name-- Who? (*About to fall to his knees.*)

BERTA. A mask.

VERRINA (*reflects in agitation, then takes a step back*). No. Can't be. Even God wouldn't give me *such* an idea. (*A shout of laughter.*) Old fop! As if all venom were spewed by one and the same toad! (*To Berta, more composed.*) My height, or shorter?

BERTA. Taller.

VERRINA (*quickly*). Black hair, curly hair?

BERTA. Coal black and curly.

VERRINA (*staggers away from her*). Oh, God. My head! My head! --And his voice?

BERTA. Hoarse. A bass voice.

VERRINA (*loudly*). What colour? No, I don't want to hear any more-- His cloak--what colour was his cloak?

BERTA. A green cloak, it seemed to me.

VERRINA (*covers his face with both hands and weaves his way to the sofa*). Don't worry. Just a bit of dizziness, Daughter. (*Drops his hands. His face is death-like.*)

BERTA (*wringing her hands*). Merciful God! That's not my father.

VERRINA (*after a pause, laughing bitterly*). Quite so, quite so. You milksop, Verrina. --The little villain lays hand on the sanctuary of the law-- that was too feeble a transgression for you. --He had to reach into the sanctuary of your bloodlines-- (*Leaps up.*) Quick! Call Nicolo-- Lead and powder! --But wait! I've thought of something different--better-- Fetch me my sword, say an Our Father. (*His hand on his forehead.*) But what am I doing?

BERTA. I'm frightened, Father.

VERRINA. Come. Sit down beside me. (*With meaning.*) Tell me, Berta-- Berta, what did that old Roman do,[25] grey like ice, when they also found his daughter--how should I put it--*also* found his daughter *so attractive?* Tell me, Berta: What did Virginius say to his mutilated daughter?

BERTA (*shuddering*). I don't know what he said.

VERRINA. You silly thing-- He didn't say *a word.* (*Stands up suddenly, seizes a sword.*) He reached for a slaughtering knife.

BERTA (*frightened, rushing into his arms*). Dear God! What are you about to do?

VERRINA (*casts the sword aside*). No! There's yet justice in Genoa!

Scene 11

As above. Sacco. Calcagno.

CALCAGNO. Quick, Verrina. Make ready. Election week[26] has just begun in this Republic. We want to reach the Signoria early to choose the new Senators. The streets are thronged. All the noblemen are streaming toward Town Hall. Won't you go with us (*mocking*) to see the triumph of our freedom?

SACCO. There's a sword on the floor. Verrina looks wild. Berta's eyes are red.

CALCAGNO. By God! I see that, too, now. Something terrible has happened, Sacco.

VERRINA (*drawing up two chairs*). Sit down, both of you.

SACCO. You are frightening us, friend.

CALCAGNO. Friend, I've never seen you like this. If Berta hadn't been weeping, I would ask: Has Genoa been lost?

VERRINA (*terrible*). Lost! Be seated.

CALCAGNO (*shocked, as both seat themselves*). Verrina! I entreat you--

VERRINA. Hear what I tell you.

CALCAGNO. Sacco, it begins to dawn on me--

VERRINA. Men of Genoa-- You both know how ancient my name is. Your forebears carried our trains. My fathers fought the battles of the State. Their wives were exemplary daughters of Genoa. *Honour* was our sole capital, passed down from father to son. --Or does someone know otherwise?

SACCO. No one.

CALCAGNO. By my Redeemer, no one.

VERRINA. I am the last of my line. My wife lies buried. This daughter is her one legacy. Men of Genoa, you are my witnesses, you know how I brought her up. Will anyone come forward with a complaint that I neglected her?

CALCAGNO. Your daughter is an example for us all.

VERRINA. My friends, I am an old man. If I lose this child, I can hope for no more. My memory will be extinguished. (*With a terrible turn.*) I *have* lost her. My line is disgraced.

BOTH (*much stirred*). God forbid. (*Berta writhes, groaning, on the sofa.*)

VERRINA. Don't despair, Daughter. These men are brave and good. If they grieve for you, there'll be bloodshed. --Don't look so shocked, gentlemen. (*Slowly, with emphasis.*) One who puts Genoa under the yoke can surely also force a girl?

BOTH (*leap to their feet, pushing back their chairs*). Gianettino Doria!

BERTA (*cries out*). May the walls fall on me! My Scipio!

Scene 12

As above. Bourgognino.

BOURGOGNINO (*excited*). On your feet, my little girl. Good news! --Noble Verrina, I come to make you arbiter of my happiness. I have long loved your daughter and never dared ask for her hand because my whole fortune was afloat on unsure boards of Coromandel.[27] My *Fortuna* has just sailed safely into port, bringing me, as they say, immense treasure. I am a rich man. Give me Berta; I'll make her happy. (*Berta covers her face. Long pause.*)

VERRINA (*carefully, to Bourgognino*). Are you inclined, young man, to toss your heart into a mud puddle?

BOURGOGNINO (*reaches for his sword, then quickly withdraws his hand*). It was her father who said that--

VERRINA. Every cad in Italy will say that. Are you satisfied with the leavings of someone else's meal?

BOURGOGNINO. Don't make me crazy, you greybeard.

CALGAGNO. Bourgognino! The greybeard speaks truth.

BOURGOGNINO (*vehement, rushing to Berta*). Truth? That I've been made a fool of by a strumpet?

CALCAGNO. Not so, Bourgognino. The *girl* is perfectly pure.

BOURGOGNINO (*holds still, astonished*). Well! As sure as I live, pure and dishonoured. That's beyond me. --They all look at one another and say nothing. Some godforsaken misdeed is quivering on their trembling tongues. I entreat you. Don't play games with my reason. *Pure*? Who said *pure*?

VERRINA. My child is guiltless.

BOURGOGNINO. Force, then. (*Seizes the sword from the floor.*) Men of Genoa! By all the sins beneath the moon! Where do I find the robber?

VERRINA. Precisely where you'll find the thief of Genoa--

(*Bourgognino freezes. Verrina paces, deep in thought, then stands still.*)

VERRINA. If I understand your sign correctly, Eternal Providence, you want to free Genoa by my Berta. (*He goes to her, slowly unwinding the mourning band from his arm. Solemnly.*) Until the heart's blood of a Doria washes this blot from your honour, no ray of daylight shall fall upon your cheek. Till then-- (*he drapes the mourning band over her*) be blinded!

(*Pause. The others gaze at him in awkward silence.*)

VERRINA (*more solemnly, his hand on Berta's head*). Cursed be the breeze that caresses you. Cursed the sleep that refreshes you. Cursed every trace of humanity that you long for in your wretchedness. Go down into the deepest vaults of my cellars. Whimper. Howl. Make time stand still with your sorrow. (*He continues, interrupted by shuddering.*) Let your life be the agonized writhing of dying vermin--the unyielding, grinding battle between being and not being. --May this curse lie upon you until the last breath has rattled from Gianettino's throat. --If not, may you drag him along after you in all eternity, until we discover where the two ends of its circle mesh.

(Long silence. Horror on every face. Verrina looks firmly and searchingly at each one.)

BOURGOGNINO. You jackal of a father! What have you done? To lay this monstrous curse upon your poor, guiltless daughter!

VERRINA. Terrible, isn't it, my tender-hearted bridegroom? (*Very significantly.*) Who among you will turn up now and natter on about cold-bloodedness and need to delay? Genoa's lot has been thrown in with my Berta's. I have delivered a father's heart over to my civic duty. Who among us is weakling enough to delay Genoa's deliverance, now that he knows that his cowardice will cost this innocent lamb endless sorrow? --That was no fool's blathering, by God. --I have taken an oath and shall show my child no mercy until one of the Dorias lies stretched on the ground, in his death throes, even if I have to think up new forms of torture, like a hangman, and if I have to smash this innocent lamb on a cannibal's rack. --They're trembling. --White as a ghost, they leer at me. --I repeat, Scipio: I hold her hostage to your tyrannicide. By this cherished thread I bind you, me, and all of us to our duty. Genoa's despot must fall, or the girl will despair. I shall not recant.

BOURGOGNINO (*throwing himself at Berta's feet*). And he shall fall--fall for Genoa, like a sacrificial animal. As surely as I shall turn this sword in Doria's heart, just as surely shall I press the bridegroom's kiss upon your lips. (*Stands up.*)

VERRINA. The first bridal couple to receive the blessing of the Furies. Join hands. You will turn your sword in Doria's heart? --Then take her; she is yours.

CALCAGNO (*kneels*). Here kneels another Genoese and lays his terrible sword at the feet of innocence. May Calcagno find his way to Heaven as certainly as his sword will find an avenue to Doria's life. (*Stands up.*)

SACCO. Last, but no less determined, Raffaele Sacco kneels. If my bright steel fails to open Berta's prison, let the ear of my Redeemer be closed against my final prayer. (*Stands up.*)

VERRINA (*cheerfully*). My friends, Genoa thanks you in my person. Go now, Daughter, happy to be the great sacrifice of our country.

BOURGOGNINO (*embraces her as she leaves*). Go. Trust in God and in Bourgognino. Berta and Genoa will be free on one and the same day. (*Berta goes out.*)

Scene 13

As above, without Berta.

CALCAGNO. Before we go any further, just one word, men of Genoa.

VERRINA. I can guess what it is.

CALCAGNO. Are we four patriots sufficient to bring down tyranny, that many-headed hydra? Shouldn't we also raise the common man? Bring the nobility onto our side?

VERRINA. I understand. Listen. I have long had a painter in my service who bends all his efforts on painting the fall of Appius Claudius[28] in fresco. Fiesco adores art, loves to find excitement in exalted scenes. We'll bring the painting to his palace and be present when he sees it. Perhaps the sight of it will rouse his genius again. --Perhaps--

BOURGOGNINO. What need of him? Double the danger, says the hero, not our helpers. I've long felt something in my breast, something unappeasable. --Now suddenly I know *what* it is. (*Leaps up heroically.*) I have a tyrant before me!

(*Curtain.*)

Act Two

Antechamber in Fiesco's palace.

Scene 1

Leonora. Arabella.

ARABELLA. No, I say. You're mistaken. Your jealousy sees everything in the worst light.

LEONORA. It was the living Julia. Don't try to fool me. *My* silhouette was on a sky-blue ribbon. This one was fiery red and of watered silk. My fate is sealed.

Scene 2

As above. Julia.

JULIA (*enters affectedly*). The Count offered me his palace to watch the procession to Town Hall. I shall find it tedious enough. While my chocolate[29] is being prepared, amuse me, Madame. (*Bella goes out, returns immediately.*)

LEONORA. Do you bid me invite company?

JULIA. Tasteless. As if I had to come here to find company. *You* will divert me, Madame. (*Walking up and down, admiring herself.*) If you can, Madame--for I oughtn't to miss anything.

ARABELLA (*maliciously*). Therefore this costly moiré, Signora? How cruel of you, just think, to deprive the opera glasses of the young dandies of such a prize! Ah! And the light playing on these pearls, it's blinding. --Why, you've plundered all the seas.

JULIA (*before a mirror*). This is a rarity for you, Mamsell? Now, tell me, Mamsell, have you also hired out your tongue to your mistress? Charming, Madame, how you let your domestics pay compliments to your guests.

LEONORA. It is my misfortune, Signora, that an indisposition diminishes my pleasure in your presence.

JULIA. An ugly incivility that makes you slow-witted and silly. Quick, now. Lively and witty. *That's* no way to captivate your husband.

LEONORA. I know but *one* way, Countess. May yours always be an appealing means.

JULIA (*choosing to ignore her*). And how you present yourself, Madame! Tut, tut! Make a greater effort also with your body. Resort to art where Nature has been stingy with you. A bit of gloss for these cheeks, which sickly suffering has discoloured. Poor creature! Like that, your little face will never find a buyer.

LEONORA (*cheerfully to Bella*). Congratulate me, my girl: Either I have not lost my Fiesco or in him I have lost nothing. (*A Servant brings in chocolate; Bella pours.*)

JULIA. You murmured something about *losing*? But, heavens! What led you ever to *take* Fiesco? --And to seek this social level, my child, where you'll necessarily be seen? And *compared*. --Upon my honour, my dear, it was either a fool or a villain who joined you to Fiesco in the first place. (*Taking her hand with pity*.) Dear creature, a man who is received in elevated circles could never be a proper match for you. (*She takes a cup of chocolate.*)

LEONORA (*smiling to Arabella*). Or he would not want to be received in the houses of these elevated circles.

JULIA. The Count has presence--worldliness--taste. It was his good fortune to make acquaintances of rank. The Count has spirit, fire. He tears himself away from the choicest company, comes home, and the wife welcomes him with workaday tenderness, douses his fires with a cold, damp kiss, portions out her caresses as at a boarding house table. The poor husband! There a radiant ideal smiles upon him--here a morose over-sensitivity revolts him. For heaven's sake, Signora. Won't he lose his reason? Or what will he choose?

LEONORA (*brings her a cup of chocolate*). You, Madame--when he has lost his reason.

JULIA. Fine. That barb into your own heart. *Tremble* for this mockery, but before you tremble, *blush* with shame!

LEONORA. That, too, you are acquainted with, Signora? But of course. It's done with powder and paint.

JULIA. Well look at that! One must stir up the little caterpillar to get one spark of mother wit from her. Enough for now. It was only in fun, Madame. Give me your hand in reconciliation.

LEONORA (*offers her hand with a meaningful look*). Imperiali-- where I am *angry*, you are calm.

JULIA. Magnanimous, in any case. And should I not be, Countess? (*Slowly and captiously.*) When I wear someone's silhouette, does it not follow that I cherish the original? Or what do you think?

LEONORA (*reddening and confused*). I beg your pardon? This conclusion is hasty, I hope.

JULIA. My opinion, too. One's *heart* has no need to call upon the senses. True feeling never takes cover behind mere trinketry.

LEONORA. Dear God! What brought *you* to such a truth?

JULIA. Compassion. Pure compassion. --For, you see, the opposite is also true. --And you still have your Fiesco. (*She gives Leonora her silhouette with a malevolent burst of laughter.*)

LEONORA (*with indignant bitterness*). My silhouette? In your possession? (*Throws herself into a chair, hurt.*) That unspeakable man.

JULIA (*triumphant*). Have I gotten even? Have I? No further pinpricks at the ready, Madame? (*Calls into the wings.*) My carriage to the door! My business is finished. (*To Leonora, stroking her chin.*) Be consoled, my child. He gave me the silhouette in a fit of madness. (*Exit.*)

Scene 3

Calcagno enters.

CALCAGNO. Imperiali went out all in a pet. And you in a state, Madonna?

LEONORA (*deeply wounded*). Unheard of! Unheard of!

CALCAGNO. Good heavens! You're not crying?

LEONORA. You friend of a monster-- Out of my sight!

CALCAGNO. Of what monster? You frighten me.

LEONORA. Of my husband. --Not so! Of Fiesco.

CALCAGNO. What must I hear?

LEONORA. Oh, just a prank. The usual for you men.

CALCAGNO (*clasps her hand fervently*). My Lady, my heart responds to injured innocence.

LEONORA (*gravely*). You are a man. --It's not for me.

CALCAGNO. Wholly for you--full of you. --If only you knew how much--how very much--

LEONORA. Man, you're lying. --You're giving assurances before you act.

CALCAGNO. I swear to you--

LEONORA. A perjury. Stop it. You'll wear out the stylus of God, who records your lies. Men! Men! If your oaths should turn into as many devils, they could storm the heavens and take away the angels of light as their prisoners.

CALCAGNO. You're not yourself, Countess. Your bitterness makes you unjust. Should the entire race be held to account for the misdeeds of a single individual?

LEONORA (*gazes at him steadily*). Look! I worshipped that race in the person of an individual; should I not detest it in him, too?

CALCAGNO. Consider, Countess-- You entrusted your heart wrongly the first time. --I could tell you where it would be in safekeeping.

LEONORA. Your kind could lie the Creator clear out of his world. --I don't want to hear another word from you.

CALCAGNO. This sentence of condemnation--you'll revoke it in *my arms* before the day is out.

LEONORA (*attentively*). Go on. In *your*--

CALCAGNO. In my arms, which open to receive a woman abandoned and to indemnify her for lost love.

LEONORA (*examines him narrowly*). Love?

CALCAGNO (*kneeling before her, with ardour*). Yes! I have pronounced it. *Love*, Madonna. You dispose over life and death. If my passion is a sin, may the two ends of virtue and vice flow into one another and Heaven and Hell congeal into a *single* damnation.

LEONORA (*taking a step backward, displeased and grand*). So that's where your sympathy was tending, you sneak? --On *one* bended knee you betray both friendship and love? Out of my sight! Detestable sex! Until now I thought you deceived only women. I *never* knew that you would turn traitor to your own kind.

CALCAGNO (*stands up, disconcerted*). My Lady--

LEONORA. It was not enough to break the sacred seal of trust. This hypocrite also had to fog the bright mirror of virtue and undertake to instruct my innocence in the fine art of oath breaking.

CALCAGNO (*quickly*). It's not oath breaking on *your* part, Madonna.

LEONORA. I understand. And my sensitivity was supposed to prejudice my feelings in your favour? *This* you didn't know: (*very grand*) that precisely the exalted misfortune of *breaking for Fiesco* ennobles a woman's heart. Go! Fiesco's disgrace *elevates* no Calcagno in my eyes. It degrades mankind. (*Rapid exit.*)

CALCAGNO (*stares after her dumbly, then strikes his forehead*). Idiot!

Scene 4
The Moor. Fiesco.

FIESCO. Who was it that just went out?

MOOR. Marquis Calcagno.

FIESCO. This handkerchief was left behind on the sofa. My wife has been here.

MOOR. She just went past me, very upset.

FIESCO. The handkerchief is damp.[30] (*Puts it into his pocket.*) Calcagno present here? Leonora upset? (*After a moment's thought, to the Moor.*) I'll want to know from you this evening what it was that happened here.

MOOR. Mamsell Bella likes to be told that she is blond. Will try and get an answer for you.

FIESCO. Thirty hours have elapsed. Have you discharged my commission?

MOOR. To a "T," Lord and Master.

FIESCO (*seats himself*). Then tell me what they're whistling about Doria and our current government?

MOOR. The most atrocious little ditties. They shudder at the very sound of "Doria." They hate Gianettino mortally. Everybody's grumbling. They say the French were Genoa's rats, that tom cat Doria ate them up and is now content with the company of mice.

FIESCO. That may be true enough. --And do they know of a dog to set upon the cat?

MOOR (*teasing*). The town whispers far and wide about a certain--a certain--Huh! Could I possibly have forgotten the name?

FIESCO (*stands up*). Idiot! That name is as *easy* to remember as it was *hard* to acquire. Is there more than one such in Genoa?

MOOR. As unlikely as two Counts of Lavagna.

FIESCO (*seating himself again*). Now that's a little something. And what are they whispering about my high living?

MOOR (*measures him carefully*). Listen, Count Lavagna. Genoa must have quite an opinion of you. They can't abide that the scion of their foremost house--full of talent and good sense--at the height of his powers and his influence--who disposes over four million pounds--the blood of princes in his veins--that a cavalier like Fiesco, whom every heart would gather round at the first signal--

FIESCO (*turns away in disgust*). To have to hear all this from a rogue--

MOOR. That Genoa's great man has gone missing at Genoa's great moment. Many regret it. Very many ridicule it. Most of them condemn you. All mourn the State that has lost you. *A Jesuit claims to have caught wind of a fox in this dressing gown.*

FIESCO. *One fox can sniff out another.* --What are they saying about my adventure with the Countess Imperiali?

MOOR. I'll choose to refrain from repeating that.

FIESCO. Out with it. The more insolent, the better. *What* are they muttering?

MOOR. They're not *muttering* anything. In the coffee houses,[31] at the billiard tables, in the inns, on the promenades--in the market--at the stock exchange, they *cry* aloud--

FIESCO. What? I order you--

MOOR (*stepping back*). That you're a fool.

FIESCO. Good. Here, take the sequins for this news. I've put on a fool's cap to make the Genoese laugh at me; I'll soon have myself shaved bald, and they'll see me play Hanswurst.[32] How did the silk merchants respond to my gifts?

MOOR (*droll*). *Fool*, they made like the condemned--

FIESCO. *Fool?* Are you out of your mind, fellow?

MOOR. Oh, sorry. I'd like to have more sequins.

FIESCO (*laughs, gives him one*). Now, like the condemned--

MOOR. Who are lying on the block and then hear themselves pardoned. They are yours, body and soul.

FIESCO. Excellent. They'll determine what the common man does.

MOOR. What a scene that was! The devil take me if I wasn't about to acquire a taste for open-handedness. They threw their arms around me like madmen, the girls seemed about to lose their heads over my father's colouring, so taken were they with my dark-of-the-moon. Almighty gold, I thought. It can even bleach a Moor.

FIESCO. A thought that's better than what hatched it. --The *words* you've carried back to me are good. Do they imply *deeds*?

MOOR. The way that rumbling skies imply a breaking storm. They're putting their heads together, forming packs, clearing their throats noisily when a stranger drifts past. A leaden atmosphere broods over all Genoa. --This discontent hangs over the Republic like heavy weather. --One blast of wind and we'll have hailstones and thunderbolts.

FIESCO. Quiet! Listen! What's that strange rumbling?

MOOR (*rushes to the window*). It's the shouting of a crowd that's coming down from Town Hall.

FIESCO. They're *electing Procurators* today. My cariole to the door! The session can't possibly be over yet. I'll go up there. It can't possibly have adjourned in good order. My sword and cloak. Where's my medal?

MOOR. My Lord, I stole it and pawned it.

FIESCO. Delightful.

MOOR. Well? Is my reward coming soon?

FIESCO. Because you didn't also take my cloak?

MOOR. Because I've turned up the thief for you.

FIESCO. The commotion's moving this way. Listen-- That's not approval, that's no celebration. (*Suddenly.*) Quick, unbar the gates to the courtyard. Something tells me-- Doria is foolhardy. The State is balancing on a knife edge. I'll bet the Signoria has erupted.

MOOR (*at the window, shouts*). What the--? They're coming down the Via Balbi[33]--a pack of thousands--halberds flashing--swords-- Aha! Senators--rushing this way--

FIESCO. It's a rising. Go out and join them. Mention my name. See to it that they come this way. (*Moor rushes downstairs.*) What reason, that busy ant, drags together laboriously an accidental gust can heap up in an instant.

Scene 5

Fiesco. Centurione, Cibo, Asserato burst into the room.

CIBO. Count, ascribe it to our anger that we enter unannounced.

CENTURIONE. I have been insulted, mortally insulted, by the Duke's nephew before the entire Signoria.

ASSERATO. Doria has defiled the Golden Book, where every Genoese nobleman is entered on a page.

CENTURIONE. That's why we're here. In me the entire nobility has been affronted. The entire nobility must have a part in my revenge. To avenge my *personal* honour I would have scant need of assistance.

CIBO. In him the entire nobility has been called out. The entire nobility must breathe fire and brimstone.

ASSERATO. The rights of the nation have been reduced to ruins. Our republican freedom has taken a deathblow.

FIESCO. You have my full attention.

CIBO. He was the twenty-ninth among the Electors, had already picked up a golden ball to vote for Procurator. Twenty-eight ballots had been collected. Fourteen were for me, as many for Lomellino. Doria's and his were still outstanding.

CENTURIONE (*quickly picks up the thread*). Were still outstanding. I voted for Cibo. Doria--conceive the wound to my honour--Doria-

ASSERATO (*also breaks in*). The likes of which we've never seen, for as long as waves have washed Genoa--

CENTURIONE (*ever more heatedly*). Doria drew his sword, which he had carried concealed under his scarlet cloak, impaled my ballot, and cried into the assembly--

CIBO. "Senators! Invalid! It's perforated! Lomellino is Procurator."

CENTURIONE. "Lomellino is Procurator," and threw his sword on the table.

ASSERATO. Cried, "Invalid!" And threw his sword on the table.

FIESCO (*after a silence*). What measures will you take?

CENTURIONE. A blow to the heart of the Republic. What measures we'll take?

FIESCO. Centurione, reeds will bend in a puff of air. Oaks require a storm. I asked your measures--

CIBO. I should have thought one would ask what measures Genoa would take.

FIESCO. Genoa? Genoa? No more of that! It's crumbling, falls to pieces wherever you grasp it. You're counting on the patricians? Perhaps because they make faces, shrug their shoulders at the mention of affairs of state? No more of them! Their heroic ardour is bound up in bales of Levantine merchandise, their souls hover anxiously over their East Indian fleet.

CENTURIONE. You should form a better opinion of our patricians. No sooner had Doria delivered his provocation than several hundred of them went flying out to the market, tearing their garments. The whole Signoria flew apart.

FIESCO (*scoffing*). The way doves fly apart when a buzzard strikes the dovecote?

CENTURIONE (*storming*). No. Like powder kegs when a fuse falls into them.

CIBO. The people, too, are all in a rage. And what can't a wild boar do when it's been shot at!

FIESCO (*laughing*). That blind, clumsy colossus that first raises a great racket with its stubby legs, threatens to gobble up everything, high and low, near and far, with gaping jaws--and then, in the end, falls over a tripwire? It's no use, Genoese. Our day as rulers of the sea is over. Genoa has fallen below its reputation. Genoa has reached that point where invincible Rome threw itself like a shuttlecock into the racket of the boy Octavius.[34] Genoa is no longer capable of freedom. Genoa needs a monarch to keep it warm. Genoa needs a sovereign, so bend a knee to the addle-brained Gianettino.

CENTURIONE (*flaring up*). When the raging elements make peace with one another and the North Pole goes leaping after the South Pole. Come, comrades!

FIESCO. Stay! Stay! What are you brooding about, Cibo?

CIBO. *Either over nothing, or over a farce that's to be called "The Earthquake."*

FIESCO (*leads them to a statue*). Look at this figure.

CENTURIONE. It's the Florentine Venus.[35] What does she have to do with anything?

FIESCO. But you find her pleasing?

CIBO. I should think so, or we're no Italians. Why would you ask just now?

FIESCO. Now, then, travel to the ends of the earth and among all the living impressions of the mould of woman single out the most successful, in which all the charms of this imagined Venus are met.

CIBO. And gain what for our trouble?

FIESCO. Then you will have put imagination at the mercy of the market-crier--

CENTURIONE (*impatient*). And gained what?

FIESCO. You'll have won Nature's age-old legal action against artists.

CENTURIONE (*irritated*). And then?

FIESCO. Then? Then? (*Begins to laugh.*) Then you'll have forgotten to notice that Genoa's freedom is going to rack and ruin.

Scene 6

Fiesco. The unrest around the palace grows louder.

FIESCO. What luck! What luck! The straw of the Republic has caught, and the flame has leaped over onto houses and towers. Right on! Right on! Let there be a general conflagration, and the gleeful wind whistle among the ruins.

Scene 7

Moor in haste. Fiesco.

MOOR. Pack after pack!

FIESCO. Throw open the gates. Admit everything that walks.

MOOR. Republicans! Republicans! Hauling their freedom by a yoke, panting like loaded oxen under the weight of their aristocratic splendour.

FIESCO. Fools, to believe that Fiesco di Lavagna would *finish* what Fiesco di Lavagna did not *begin*. The *rising* comes like a godsend. But the *conspiracy* must be my work. They're storming up the steps.

MOOR (*into the stairwell*). Holla! Holla! Everyone kindly come in at the door. (*The people come storming in. The door reduced to rubble.*)

Scene 8

Fiesco. Twelve Artisans.

ALL. Revenge on Doria! Revenge on Gianettino!

FIESCO. *Easy, easy*, my compatriots. That you wait upon me *this way* testifies to your pure hearts. But my ears are more delicate.

ALL (*more agitated*). Down with the Dorias! With uncle and nephew alike!

FIESCO (*smiling, counting them*). Twelve are an eminent army--

SOME. These Dorias must go. The State must take a different form.

FIRST ARTISAN. To throw our magistrates down the stairs--our magistrates down the stairs!

SECOND ARTISAN. Think of it, Lavagna, down the stairs, when they contradicted him about the election.

ALL. Not to be tolerated! Cannot be tolerated!

A THIRD ARTISAN. To bring a sword into Council--

FIRST ARTISAN. A sword! The sign of war! In the hall of peace!

SECOND ARTISAN. To come into the Senate wearing scarlet! Not black, like the other councillors!

Act Two 45

FIRST ARTISAN. To drive eight stallions straight through the middle of our capital.

ALL. A tyrant! A traitor to the country and to the government!

SECOND ARTISAN. To buy two hundred German soldiers from the Emperor for his bodyguard--

FIRST ARTISAN. Foreigners against the children of the fatherland! Germans against Italians! Soldiers, in addition to the laws!

ALL. High treason! Mutiny! The end of Genoa!

FIRST ARTISAN. To carry the blazon of the Republic on his carriage--

SECOND ARTISAN. And the statue of Andrea in the very middle of the courtyard of the Signoria!

ALL. Smash him to pieces--the stone Andrea and the living one.

FIESCO. Genoese, why bring all this to *me*?

FIRST ARTISAN. You shouldn't stand for it. You should hold your thumbs on his eyes.

SECOND ARTISAN. You're a smart man and shouldn't stand for it and ought to sympathize with us.

FIRST ARTISAN. And a better nobleman and should put it to him, and you ought not stand for it.

FIESCO. I'm flattered by your confidence in me. Can I deserve it by deeds?

ALL (*noisily*). Strike! Throw down! Set free!

FIESCO. You'll hear a word of caution?

SOME. Tell us, Lavagna.

FIESCO (*seating himself*). Genoese-- Unrest once broke out among the citizens of the Animal Kingdom.[36] One side went to war against the other and a *butcher's dog* seized the throne. It was his custom to drive the animals to slaughter, so he lived like a dog in his kingdom, barked, bit, and gnawed at the bones of his people. The nation grumbled; the boldest ones came together and strangled their princely bulldog. They convened a council of state to decide a great question: what the best form of government would be. Opinion was divided three ways. Genoese, what form would you have chosen?

FIRST CITIZEN. By the people, by the people.

FIESCO. The people won. The government became democratic. Every citizen cast a vote. The *majority* prevailed. After a few weeks, Man declared war on the fresh-baked free state. The state held a convention. The Horse, Lion, Tiger, Bear, Elephant, and Rhinoceros came forward and bellowed: To arms! Then it was the turn of the others. The Lamb, Hare, Stag, Donkey, the entire world of insects, the whole shy army of birds and fishes--all intervened and wailed: Peace! Behold, Genoese: The cowardly were *more* numerous than the battle-ready, the stupid *more* numerous than the smart ones. --The *majority* prevailed. The Animal Kingdom laid down its arms, and Man plundered its territory. So this system was abandoned. What would have been your preference now, Genoese?

FIRST AND SECOND CITIZENS. The committee! Yes, of course, the committee!

FIESCO. That found favour. The affairs of state were divided into several chambers. *Wolves* saw to finance, *foxes* became their secretaries. *Doves* took charge of criminal justice, *tigers* of pleas and settlements, *billy goats* heard domestic disputes. The *hares* became soldiers, *lions* and *elephant* guarded the baggage train, the Donkey was the state ambassador, and the Mole oversaw the administration of the departments. Genoese, what hopes have you of this wise division? What the Wolf didn't tear apart, the Fox did in. What escaped the Fox, the Donkey knocked over. Tigers throttled the innocent, the Dove pardoned thieves and murderers, and in the end, when all had laid down their offices, the Mole found them to have been lawfully exercised. --The animals rebelled. Let us choose a *monarch*, they cried unanimously, who has claws and a brain and only *one* belly. --And they all declared allegiance to *one* lord--*one*, Genoese. --But (*going among them majestically*) it was the Lion.

ALL (*clap, toss their caps into the air*). Bravo! Bravo! That was clever.

FIRST CITIZEN. And Genoa should do the same and already has its man.

FIESCO. I don't want to know who. Go home now and think about the Lion. (*The Citizens go tumbling out.*) Just what I wanted. People and

Senate against Doria. People and Senate for Fiesco. --Hassan! Hassan! --I must catch this breeze. --Hassan! Hassan! --I must fan this hate, keep this interest alive. --Show yourself, Hassan! Whoreson of Hell! Hassan! Hassan!

Scene 9

Moor enters. Fiesco.

MOOR (*wild*). My feet are on fire. What now?

FIESCO. What I command.

MOOR (*smoothly*). Where would you have me run first, where last?

FIESCO. You can spare yourself the running this time. You're going to be dragged. Steel yourself. I'm going to trumpet your attempted murder abroad and turn you over, bound, to the criminal Rota.[37]

MOOR (*six steps backward*). My Lord? --That's contrary to our agreement!

FIESCO. Keep calm. It's pure farce. At the moment everything depends on *making Gianettino's attempt on my life a public scandal.* You'll be questioned under torture.

MOOR. Do I confess or deny?

FIESCO. Deny. They'll put you on the rack. You'll withstand the first turn of the screw. That bit of edification you can mark up to your assassination attempt. On the second turn, you confess.

MOOR (*shakes his head, dubious*). The Devil is a knave. The gentlemen could detain me for further edification and dismember me for their amusement.

FIESCO. You'll get away whole. I give you my word as a nobleman. I'll request the satisfaction of punishing you myself and then pardon you before the whole Republic.

MOOR. Fine. I'll do it. They'll disjoint me. That'll limber me up.

FIESCO. Then take your dagger and cut a quick stripe in my arm until you draw blood. I'll pretend I've just caught you in the act. --Good!

(*Shrieking.*) Murder! Murder! Murder! Block the passages! Bar the gates! (*He drags the Moor out by the throat. Servants rush over the set.*)

Scene 10

Leonora, Rosa run in, frightened.

LEONORA. Murder, they cried, murder! It came from here.

ROSA. Some pointless uproar, like every day in Genoa.

LEONORA. They cried murder, and I clearly heard the people saying "Fiesco." Wretched deceivers. They tried to keep me from seeing, but my heart outwitted them. Quick, go after them. Look and see, then come tell me where they're taking him.

ROSA. Calm yourself. Bella has gone.

LEONORA. Bella will receive his dying glance. Happy Bella! Wretched woman that I am, his assassin! If Fiesco had been able to love me, he would never have thrown himself into the world, never have thrown himself onto the daggers of envy. --Bella's coming! Oh, go away! Don't tell me anything, Bella!

Scene 11

As above. Bella.

BELLA. The Count is alive and unhurt. I saw him galloping through town. I never saw our Gracious Master more handsome. His black stallion bore him magnificently, its haughty hooves frightened the pressing crowd back away from its princely rider. He caught sight of me as he flew past, smiled graciously, gestured this way, and tossed back three kisses. (*With malice.*) What shall I do with them, Signora?

LEONORA (*enchanted*). You silly chatterbox! Bring them back to him.

ROSA. There, you see? You're blushing again to the eyebrows.

LEONORA. He throws away his heart on strumpets, and I chase after a single glance? --Oh, women! Women!

(*All leave the scene.*)

Scene 12

The palace of Andrea Doria.
Gianettino, Lomellino enter hastily.

GIANETTINO. They may bawl after their freedom the way the lioness bawls after her young. I'm not budging.

LOMELLINO. But, my Gracious Lord--

GIANETTINO. Go to the devil with your *But*, you Procurator of three hours' duration. Not one inch. Genoa's towers may shake their heads and the wild sea roar *No* in among them. I'm not afraid of that pack.

LOMELLINO. The mob is the tinder, of course, but the nobility is wind on the flames. The whole Republic is in uproar--the people and the patricians.

GIANETTINO. Then I, like Nero,[38] will stand on a hilltop and watch this farcical blaze--

LOMELLINO. Until the whole mass of the insurrection throws itself behind a partisan ambitious enough to reap in the destruction.

GIANETTINO. Antics! Antics! I know only one man whom one might *possibly* fear and he's taken care of.

LOMELLINO. His Grace! (*Andrea enters. Gianettino and Lomellino bow deeply.*)

ANDREA. Signor Lomellino. My niece wishes to drive out.

LOMELLINO. It will be my privilege to accompany her. (*Exit.*)

Scene 13

Andrea. Gianettino.

ANDREA. Hear me, Nephew. I am ill-content with you.

GIANETTINO. Uncle-- May Your Grace grant me a hearing.

ANDREA. Granted to the most ragged beggar in Genoa, if he's worth something. Never to a knave, and were he my nephew. It's grace enough that I come before you as your uncle; it's the Duke you've deserved to hear from, and his Signoria.

GIANETTINO. Just one word, most Gracious Lord--

ANDREA. *You* hear what you have done and then answer for it. --You have ripped down an edifice that I constructed painstakingly over the course of half a century--your uncle's mausoleum, his one pyramid: the love of the Genoese. *That* bit of foolishness Andrea forgives you.

GIANETTINO. My uncle and Duke--

ANDREA. Don't interrupt me. You have damaged the finest work of art of my rule, that *I personally* fetched from Heaven for the Genoese, that cost me so many sleepless nights, so much danger and so much blood. Before all Genoa you have defiled my princely honour, by showing no respect for *my* institution. Who will find it sacred if *my own blood* despises it? --This *stupidity* your uncle forgives you.

GIANETTINO (*insulted*). Most Gracious Lord, you brought me up to be Genoa's Duke.

ANDREA. Silence! --You've committed high treason and struck at the heart of the State. Take note, boy. The watchword is: Submission! --Just because the shepherd has stepped back in the evening of his day's work, did you think the flock had been abandoned? Because Andrea's hair had turned icy grey, you could trample on the laws like a street urchin?

GIANETTINO (*defiant*). Come now, Duke. Even in *my* veins Andrea's blood runs hot--Andrea, before whom France trembled.

ANDREA. Silence! I give orders here. --I'm accustomed to the sea falling silent when I speak. --You spat upon the majesty of Justice in her very temple. Do you know the penalty for that, you rebel? --Answer me!

(*Gianettino stares silently at the floor.*)

ANDREA. Unhappy Andrea! In your own bosom you have hatched the *worm* that will devour your achievement. I built the Genoese a house that I intended to scorn the passage of time--and I throw the *first torch* into it: this one here. You vandal, you may thank my grey head, which wishes to be laid in the grave by family hands--thank my godless love, that I don't toss the insulted State the head of this insurrectionist from the blood-soaked boards of the scaffold. (*Exit at speed.*)

Scene 14

Lomellino, breathless, frightened. Gianettino glowers after the Duke, speechless.

LOMELLINO. What I've seen! What I've heard! Flee, Prince, this very minute. All is lost.

GIANETTINO (*furious*). What was there to lose?

LOMELLINO. Genoa, Prince. I've just come from the market. The people were thronging around a Moor who was being dragged along on cords-- Count Lavagna and over three hundred noblemen after him into the law courts, where criminals are tortured. The Moor had been caught in an assassination attempt on Fiesco.

GIANETTINO (*stamps his foot*). What? Has all Hell broken loose today?

LOMELLINO. He was put under sharp interrogation, wouldn't confess who had hired him. They put him to the first torture. He wouldn't confess. They put him to the second. He confessed--he confessed-- My Gracious Lord, whatever were you thinking when you staked your honour on a good-for-nothing?

GIANETTINO (*snorts at him*). Don't question me!

LOMELLINO. Then hear the rest. No sooner had the word "Doria" been pronounced--I would rather have seen my name on the Devil's roll than heard yours there--than Fiesco showed himself to the crowd. You know him: the man who, giving orders, seems to be appealing, who exploits the feelings of the mob. The whole assembled company, standing breathless and frozen in menacing groups, leaned toward him, listening. He spoke only briefly, then uncovered his bleeding arm, and the people fought over the falling drops as over relics. The Moor was released into his custody, and Fiesco--a fatal blow for us--Fiesco pardoned him. The silent crowd broke into a roar, every breath drawn destroyed a Doria, and Fiesco was carried home by thousands cheering in chorus.

GIANETTINO (*with stifled laughter*). Let the clamour swell to the level of my throat! --Emperor *Charles*:[39] with this one syllable I'll flatten them, and no bell will ever toll again in Genoa.

LOMELLINO. Bohemia lies far from Italy. --If Charles hurries, he'll be here in time for your funeral banquet.

GIANETTINO (*produces a letter with a large seal*). A good thing he is already here! --Lomellino is surprised? Did he think me foolhardy enough to tease raging Republicans if they had not already been sold out and betrayed?

LOMELLINO (*startled*). I don't know what I think.

GIANETTINO. I think something that you don't know. The decision is made. Day after tomorrow, twelve Senators will die. Doria will become monarch and Emperor Charles will protect him. --You step back?

LOMELLINO. Twelve Senators? My heart isn't ample enough to grasp a twelvefold bloodguilt.

GIANETTINO. You dunce, they'll be undone at the throne. Look, with Charles's ministers I considered that France still has strong partisans in Genoa, who could play it into French hands again if they're not destroyed root and branch. That worried old Charles. He subscribed to my plot. --And *you* are going to write what I dictate.

LOMELLINO. I don't yet know--

GIANETTINO. Sit down. Write.

LOMELLINO. What am I to write? (*Sits down.*)

GIANETTINO. The names of our twelve candidates. --Francesco Centurione.

LOMELLINO (*writes*). As thanks for his vote, he gets to lead the funeral procession.

GIANETTINO. Cornelio Calva.

LOMELLINO. Calva.

GIANETTINO. Michele Cibo.

LOMELLINO. That'll cool off the Procuratoria.

GIANETTINO. Tommaso Asserato and three brothers. (*Lomellino hesitates.*)

GIANETTINO (*with emphasis*). And three brothers.

LOMELLINO (*writing*). Go on.

GIANETTINO. Fiesco di Lavagna.

LOMELLINO. Watch out! Watch out! You'll break your neck yet on this black slate.[40]

GIANETTINO. Scipio Bourgognino.

LOMELLINO. Let him celebrate his wedding elsewhere.

GIANETTINO. Where *I* shall lead in the bride. Raffaele Sacco.

LOMELLINO. I ought to procure an amnesty for him until he's paid back my five thousand scudi. (*Writes.*) Death cancels all debts.

GIANETTINO. Vinzenco Calcagno.

LOMELLINO. Calcagno. --I'll write the twelfth at my *own* risk, or we've forgotten our mortal enemy.

GIANETTINO. All's well that ends well. Giovanni Verrina.

LOMELLINO. That's the dragon's head. (*Stands up, strews sand, scans the list, hands it to the Prince.*) Death is holding a great gala day after tomorrow and has invited twelve Genoese princes.

GIANETTINO (*steps to the table, signs*). It is done. --Two days from now we elect a Doge. When the Signoria has assembled, the twelve will be cut down by a *single* sudden volley at the signal of a handkerchief; simultaneously, my two hundred Germans will take Town Hall by storm. Once that's done, Gianettino Doria enters the hall and receives their obeisance. (*Rings.*)

LOMELLINO. And Andrea?

GIANETTINO (*contemptuously*). Is an *old, old* man. (*A Servant.*) If the Duke asks, I am at Mass. (*Servant leaves.*) The devil in me requires a saint's mask to keep his incognito.

LOMELLINO. And the list, Prince?

GIANETTINO. Is for you to take and circulate among our partisans. This letter is to go by express to Levanto.[41] It informs Spinola[42] of everything and summons him to enter the capital at eight in the morning. (*About to leave.*)

LOMELLINO. There's a leak in the keg, Prince. Fiesco no longer appears in the Senate.

GIANETTINO (*over his shoulder*). There'll still be *one* assassin abroad in Genoa? --I'll take care of that. (*Exit to one side, Lomellino to the other.*)

Scene 15

Antechamber in Fiesco's palace.
Fiesco with letters and bills of exchange. Moor.

FIESCO. Four galleys in port, then.

MOOR. Lying safely before anchor in the Darsena.[43]

FIESCO. Just when they're wanted. The express letters are from where?

MOOR. Rome, Piacenza, and France.[44]

FIESCO (*breaks the seals, reads rapidly*). Welcome, welcome to Genoa. (*Very content.*) *Princely* accommodation for the couriers.

MOOR. Hm! (About to go.)

FIESCO. Wait! Wait! Here's plenty of work for you.

MOOR. What're your orders? The nose of a tracking dog? The sting of a scorpion?

FIESCO. For the moment, the sound of a bird lure. Tomorrow morning two thousand men will slip into the city under cover to take service with me. Station your henchmen around the gates with orders to keep a keen eye on travellers entering. Some will come as a company of pilgrims to Loretto,[45] others as friars or Savoyards or travelling players, still others as merchants or as a troupe of musicians, most of them as discharged soldiers who want to eat Genoese bread. Every stranger is to be asked where he is put up. If he answers: *At the sign of the Golden Snake,* he is to be welcomed and shown the way to my home. Listen, fellow, I'm counting on your cleverness.

MOOR. As on my wickedness, Master. If one lock of hair escapes me, you should load my two eyes into an air musket and shoot sparrows with them. (*About to leave.*)

FIESCO. Stop! Another job. The galleys are going to attract the attention of the whole nation. Make note of what is said about them. If you're asked, then you heard a *distant rumour* that your master is going to chase Turks with them. You understand?

MOOR. Understood. The beards of the circumcised[46] are lying on top--what's *in* the basket the devil only knows. (*Again about to leave.*)

FIESCO. Not so fast. One more precaution. Gianettino has new grounds for hating me and laying traps. Observe your comrades for any sign of an assassination in the making. Doria visits doubtful houses. Keep company with the ladies of the night. The secrets of the privy council like to conceal themselves in the folds of women's skirts. Promise them customers who spit gold, promise them your master. Nothing is so sacred that you shouldn't plunge it into this morass until you hit firm bottom.

MOOR. Wait! Aha! I'm received by a certain Diana Bononi and have been supplying her for five quarters now. Day before yesterday I saw Procurator Lomellino coming out of her house.

FIESCO. Just what we need. Precisely this Lomellino is the master key to all Doria's wild schemes. You must go there early tomorrow. He may be playing Endymion to that chaste Luna[47] this very night.

MOOR. One circumstance, my Lord. When the Genoese ask--and the devil take me, they will--when they ask: What does Fiesco think on the subject of Genoa? --Are you going to wear your mask a while longer, or what should I answer?

FIESCO. Answer? Wait! The fruit is surely ready. And pangs announce the birth. You should answer: Genoa is lying on the block and your master's name is Gian Luigi Fiesco.

MOOR (*stretches himself contentedly*). Which I intend to impart to excellent effect, by my honour as a scoundrel. --But now, look sharp, friend Hassan. First, into a tavern. My feet have their hands full--I must stroke my belly, so that it puts in a good word with my legs. (*Hurries out, and comes back immediately.*) By the way, I almost forgot. You wanted to know what happened between your wife and Calcagno? --He got the gate, that's what he got. (*Runs off.*)

Scene 16

Fiesco alone.

FIESCO. My regrets, Calcagno. --Did you think I would have exposed so sensitive an article as my marriage bed, had *my wife's virtue* and *my own worth* not been warranty enough for me? Nevertheless, welcome into the family. You're a good soldier, and that should secure me your arm in destroying Doria. (*Pacing with long strides.*) Now, Doria, with me onto the battlefield! All the machinery for this great exploit is in motion. All instruments tuned for a shuddering concert. All I need do now is rip off the mask and show the Genoese patriots Fiesco. (*Sound of approaching footsteps.*) Company! Who comes now?

Scene 17

Enter Verrina, Romano with a picture, Sacco, Bourgognino, Calcagno. All bow.

FIESCO (*coming to meet them, in high spirits*). Welcome, my worthy friends. What important matter brings you to me in such numbers? --You here, too, valued Verrina? I would no longer know you, were you not more present in my thoughts than before my eyes. Have I not lived in want of my Verrina since the last ball?

VERRINA. Don't hold him to account, Fiesco. Heavy burdens have bent his grey head in the meantime. But enough of that.

FIESCO. Not enough for inquiring love. You'll have to tell me more when we're alone. (*To Bourgognino.*) Welcome, my young hero. Our acquaintanceship is yet *green*, but my friendship is fully ripe. Have you raised your estimation of me?

BOURGOGNINO. I've well begun to.

FIESCO. Verrina, they tell me this young knight is to become your son-in-law. I applaud your choice. Though I've spoken with him only once, I would be proud to have him as my own.

VERRINA. This judgment makes me vain about my daughter.

FIESCO (*to the others*). Sacco? Calcagno? --Such rare presences in my halls! Almost enough to make me ashamed of my wish to be useful, if Genoa's noblest ornaments do not call upon it. --And here I welcome a fifth guest, unknown to me, yet commended enough by this worthy circle.

ROMANO. It is a mere painter, my Gracious Lord, Romano by name, who supports himself by stealing from Nature, carries no coat of arms but his brush, and now comes before you (*with a deep bow*) in search of the great line for a portrait of Brutus.[48]

FIESCO. Give me your hand, Romano. Your mistress is a kinswoman of my house. I love her as a brother. *Art* is the *right hand* of Nature. *She* has made only *creatures*, art has made *men*. What do you paint, Romano?

ROMANO. Scenes from sinewy Antiquity. My *Dying Hercules* is in Florence, my *Cleopatra* in Venice, my *Mad Ajax* in Rome, where the heroes of the ancient world--are being resurrected in the Vatican.

FIESCO. And how is your brush now engaged?

ROMANO. I have thrown it away, my Gracious Lord. The *lamp of genius* was receiving less oil than the *lamp of life*. Beyond a certain point, only the candle's *paper collar* burns. This is my final work.

FIESCO (*expansive*). It could not have come at a better moment. I am in unusually good spirits today, all my being marks and observes a certain heroic tranquillity, wholly receptive to the beauties of Nature. Set up your picture. I shall make a feast of it. Gather round, friends. We want to give ourselves over to the artist entirely. Set up your picture.

VERRINA (*signals the others*). Now take note, Genoese.

ROMANO (*sets the picture to rights*). The light must come from *this* side. Raise the drapery over *there*, *here* let it fall. Good. (*He steps aside.*) It is the story of Virginia, and of Appius Claudius.[49]

(*Long, expressive pause as all observe the picture.*)

VERRINA (*in transports*). Strike, you ice-grey father. --Are you twitching, tyrant? --How ghastly pale you stand there, Roman blockheads. --Follow him, Romans. --His slaughtering knife is flashing. --Follow me, Genoese blockheads. --Down with Doria! Down! Down! (*He strikes at the picture.*)

FIESCO (*smiling at the Painter*). Do you require a greater tribute? Your art has made a beardless dreamer of this old man.

VERRINA (*exhausted*). Where am I? What's become of them? Vanished, like soap bubbles? You here, Fiesco? Is the tyrant still alive, Fiesco?

FIESCO. Can you see? Lost in looking, you've forgotten your eyes. You find this head of a Roman admirable? Not a bit of it. Look here at the girl. Her expression, how soft, how womanly! How much loveliness slips away through these fading lips! What ecstasy in her eyes' dying light! --Inimitable! God-like, Romano! --And this dazzling white bosom, how deliciously it swells on the last surge of breath! More such nymphs, Romano, and I shall kneel before your fantasies and send Nature a bill of divorce.

BOURGOGNINO. Is that the effect you hoped for, Verrina?

VERRINA. Take courage, Son. God has rejected Fiesco's arm; he must be counting on *ours*.

FIESCO (*to the Painter*). Yes, Romano, it's your last work. Your best powers are exhausted. You'll never touch another paintbrush. But in my admiration for the artist I forget to devour the work. I could stand here gaping and not even hear an earthquake. Take your picture away. To pay for this portrait of Virginia I would have to mortgage all Genoa. Take it away.

ROMANO. Honour is the painter's compensation. I present it to you as a gift. (*He moves to leave.*)

FIESCO. Just a moment, Romano. (*He paces the room majestically and seems to be reflecting on something of magnitude. He glances occasionally at the others, fleetingly and attentively; finally he takes the Painter by the hand and leads him before the picture.*) Step here, painter. (*Very proud and dignified.*) You stand here so boldly because you simulate *life* on *dead* canvas and memorialize great deeds at small cost. You claim fame with such heat as poets muster, with fantasy's marrowless puppet play, without heart, without the power to create warm-blooded deeds. You bring down tyrants on canvas--and are yourself a miserable slave? You liberate republics with a paintbrush--and cannot break your own chains? (*Full-throated and commanding.*) Go! --Your work is sleight of hand. --Let *appearances* yield to *deeds*. (*Grandly, tossing over the picture.*) *I have done* what you--only painted. (*All are shaken. Romano carries off his picture, deeply startled.*)

Scene 18

Fiesco. Verrina. Bourgognino. Sacco. Calcagno.

FIESCO (*breaks a stunned silence*). Did you think the lion was asleep just because he wasn't roaring? Were you conceited enough to persuade yourselves that you alone felt Genoa's chains? That you alone wanted to break them? Before you even heard them rattling in the distance, Fiesco had shattered them. (*He opens the casket, removes a packet of letters that he spreads over the table top.*) Here, soldiers from Parma--here, French money--here, four galleys from the Pope. What more is needed to flush a tyrant off his nest? What more can you think to add? (*Frozen silence. He steps away from the table; with self-assurance.*) Republicans! You're more adroit at cursing tyrants than at blowing them up. (*All except Verrina throw themselves, speechless, at Fiesco's feet.*)

VERRINA. Fiesco! --I bend my spirit before yours. --But not my knee. You are a great man--but-- Stand up, Genoese.

FIESCO. All Genoa raged about that weakling Fiesco. All Genoa swore over the philandering cad Fiesco. Genoese! My philandering deceived that cunning despot, my *madness* concealed my dangerous *good wits* from your inquisitiveness. The stupendous work of the conspiracy lay swaddled in the wrappings of wantonness. Enough! In you Genoa knows me for who I am. My most monstrous desire has been satisfied.

BOURGOGNINO (*throws himself crossly into a chair*). Do I count for nothing anymore?

FIESCO. But let us move quickly from thoughts to deeds. All the machinery is in place. I can storm the city from land and sea. Rome, France, and Parma are giving me cover. The nobility is angry. I have the heart of the common man. I have lulled the tyrants to sleep. The Republic is ripe to be recast. We are done with mere luck. Nothing is lacking-- But Verrina is lost in thought?

BOURGOGNINO. One moment. I have a quick word that will rouse him faster than the trumpets of the Last Judgment. (*He approaches Verrina and calls significantly.*) Father, wake up! Your Berta is despairing!

VERRINA. Who said that! --To work, Genoese!

FIESCO. Consider now how we shall accomplish all this. Night has overtaken our first consultation. All Genoa lies sleeping. The tyrant falls into bed, exhausted by the day's bad deeds. Wake and watch for both.

BOURGOGNINO. Before we separate, let us consecrate our heroic alliance by an embrace. (*They link arms and form a circle.*) Genoa's five greatest hearts here become one to decide Genoa's greatest lot. (*They press closer.*) When the universal order falls apart and the pronouncement of the Last Judgment cuts the bonds of blood and love, this heroic five-fold blade will remain entire! (*They separate.*)

VERRINA. When do we meet again?

FIESCO. Tomorrow at noon I'll hear your opinions.

VERRINA. Tomorrow noon, then. Good night, Fiesco. Come, Bourgognino. I have something strange to tell you. (*Both depart.*)

FIESCO (*to the others*). Go out by the rear gates, so that Doria's spies don't notice anything. (*All depart.*)

Scene 19

Fiesco, pacing thoughtfully.

FIESCO. What a commotion in my breast! ---What a secret flight of thoughts. Like suspect brothers setting out on some black deed, who walk on tiptoe and fearfully turn their burning gaze to the ground--thus do wanton phantoms flit past my inner eye. --Stop! Stop! Let me hold a light up to your face. --A good thought steals a man's heart and shows itself heroically in broad daylight. --Aha! I know you! --That's the livery of the Eternal Liar.[50] --Be gone! (*Pause, then more animated.*) *Republican Fiesco? Duke Fiesco?* --Careful. --This is the steep precipice that closes off the borderland of virtue, where Heaven and Hell take separate ways. --Just here heroes have foundered and heroes have sunk, and the world besets their name with curses. --Here, too, heroes have hesitated, heroes have halted and then gone on to become demigods--(*Gathering speed.*) That they should be *mine*, the hearts of Genoa? That terrible Genoa should let itself be twitched first here, then there by lead strings in *my* hands? --Oh, the sly sin that conceals every devil behind an angel. --Disastrous ambition! Ancient enticement! In your embrace angels kissed away Heaven, and Death sprang from your labouring loins. (*Shakes himself, shuddering.*) You snared angels with your siren song of eternity. You fish for men with lures of gold, women, and crowns! (*After a thoughtful pause, firmly.*) To capture a diadem is *great*. To toss one aside is *god-like*. (Resolutely.) Perish, Tyrant! Be free, Genoa, and I (*with devotion*) your *happiest* citizen!

Act Three

Frightful wilderness.

Scene 1

Verrina, Bourgognino come through the night.

BOURGOGNINO (*stands still*). But where are you leading me, Father? In your laboured breathing I still hear the dull pain that prompted you to call me away. Break this horrible silence. Speak. I'll go no farther.

VERRINA. This is the place.

BOURGOGNINO. The most terrible you could have found. If what you undertake here resembles this place, Father, my hair will stand on end.

VERRINA. But this is a *garden* compared with the night of my soul. Follow me to where decay eats at corpses until they have rotted away and death celebrates its horrible banquet--where the whimpering of lost souls makes devils laugh, and the thankless tears of wretchedness drain from the riddled sieve of eternity-- there, my Son, where the world changes its password and the Godhead breaks its escutcheon of benignity. --There I'll speak to you in *distortions,* and you will hear me over chattering teeth.

BOURGOGNINO. Hear? What? I entreat you.

VERRINA. Young man, I fear-- Young man, your blood is red as roses--your flesh is sweetly supple. The feelings of *such* a temperament are tender and human. My frightful knowledge melts away in the warmth of this sensitive flame. If the frosts of old age or its leaden sorrow had stilled your leaping spirits--if the clotted black blood of suffering Nature had blocked the way to your heart, then you would be able to understand the language of my grief and to contemplate, with amazement, what I have decided.

BOURGOGNINO. I shall hear it and make it *my own*.

VERRINA. Not for that reason, my Son. Verrina will spare your heart that. Oh, Scipio, a heavy burden weighs upon my breast--a thought as hideous as night that shuns the day--monstrous enough to burst a man's breast. --Do you understand? I intend to *execute* it *alone*, but *bear* it *alone* I cannot. If I were a proud man, Scipio, I could say that it is a torment to be the *one great man*. --Even the Creator found *greatness* too much and made spirits into his trusted friends. --Hear, Scipio--

BOURGOGNINO. My soul is entirely open to yours.

VERRINA. Hear and make no reply. Not a word, young man. Do you hear? Not one word should you answer. *Fiesco must die*!

BOURGOGNINO (*dismayed*). Die? Fiesco?

VERRINA. Die! --I thank you, God. Now it is said. --Fiesco must die, Son, and by my hand. --Now go. --There are deeds that submit to no human judgment--that recognize only Heaven as their arbiter. --This is such a one. Go. I want neither your praise nor your blame. I know what it will cost me and that is enough. But listen--you could go mad just thinking about it--listen: Did you see him yesterday preening before the mirror of our consternation? --The man whose smile misled all Italy--do you think he'd tolerate another such in Genoa? --Go. Fiesco will bring down the tyrant. That is certain. And Fiesco will become Genoa's most dangerous tyrant. That is more certain still! (*Rapid exit. Bourgognino gazes after him, astonished and speechless, then follows him slowly.*)

Scene 2

A hall in Fiesco's palace.
In the middle of the back wall a large glass door opens a prospect over
the sea and Genoa. Dawn.

FIESCO (*at the window*). What to make of this? --The moon is down. --Morning rises fiery from the sea. --Wild fantasies have consumed my sleep--have coiled all my being tightly around a *single* feeling. --I need to stretch myself in the open air. (*He opens the glass door. Sea and city flaming in the dawn light. Paces the room with long strides.*) That I'm the greatest man in all Genoa? Shouldn't smaller souls then gather under the great one? --Or am I offending against virtue? (*Stands still.*) Virtue? --The exalted head knows other temptations than the ordinary one. --Should it be bound by the same virtue as the other? --The armour that constrains a pygmy's puny body--should *it* have to fit a giant's limbs?

(The sun rises over Genoa.)

This majestic city. (*Rushing toward it with open arms.*) Mine! --And then to rise flaming over it like regal day? --Hover over it with monarchic power? --And plunge all this seething desire-- all these unappeasable longings into that bottomless ocean? --Why, yes! Even if the deceiver's wit does not ennoble the deception, nonetheless the prize ennobles the deceiver. It is shameful to empty a purse--cheeky to embezzle a million, but indescribably great to steal a crown. The ignominy *diminishes* as the sin *grows greater*. (*Pause. Then expressively.*) To obey! --To rule! --Immense, vertiginous gap. --Throw into it all that man considers most valuable: your battles won, conquerors-- artists, your deathless works--your pleasures, Epicureans--your seas and islands, you explorers. *To obey and to rule! --Being and Nothingness!* One who sets out over the bottomless moat of the last seraph to reach the Unbounded and Eternal will be able to measure this leap, too. (*Exalted gestures.*) To stand on that frighteningly lofty height--and smile down into the racing maelstrom of humanity, where the wheel of Fortune, that blind deceiver, turns perfidiously--to drink first from joy's cup--to pull that armoured giant, *Law*, far below, along on lead strings--to see wounds struck unpunished while its short-armed anger bangs helplessly on the parapets of majesty--to master the unruly passions of the people, like so many plunging horses, by a light touch on the reins--to lay the vassals' prideful ambition in the dust with *one* breath--one breath--even while the prince's creative staff lifts his princely fever dreams into life. --What a picture! It flings the astonished spirit over its own boundaries! --*One* moment as *prince* and the marrow of all existence is consumed. It is not the *arena* of life--its *substance* is what determines its worth. Pick thunder apart into its separate syllables and you can sing children to sleep with it; forge them into a *single* sudden noise, and that monarchical sound will shake the eternal heavens. --I am resolved! (*Walking heroically up and down.*)

Scene 3

Fiesco. Leonora enters, visibly anxious.

LEONORA. Forgive me, Count. I'm afraid I'm disturbing your morning.

FIESCO (*steps back, very abashed*). Indeed, my Lady. This is quite a surprise.

LEONORA. Only to lovers does this never happen.

FIESCO. Lovely Countess, you're exposing your beauty to the injurious morning air.

LEONORA. Yet I wouldn't know why I should save the little that's left of it for sorrow and regret.

FIESCO. *Sorrow*, my love? Did I ever imagine that not wanting *to overturn the State* amounted to peace of mind?

LEONORA. Possibly. --But I still feel my woman's heart break under this peace of mind. I have come, my Lord, to burden you with a trivial request, if you can spare the time for me. For the last seven months I have dreamed, strangely, that I was the Countess Lavagna. That dream has vanished. And my head aches. To heal my spirits of this vivid imagining I shall have to summon all the happiness of my innocent childhood. Will you therefore permit me to return to the arms of my kind mother?

FIESCO (*deeply startled*). Countess?

LEONORA. My heart is a feeble, coddled thing, and you must have pity on it. Even the least reminder of that dream could harm my ailing fancy. Therefore I return these last remaining pledges to their rightful owner. (*She lays a handful of love tokens on a little table.*) And this dagger that pierced my heart (*his love letter*). --This one, too (*she is about to rush from the room, weeping loudly*)--and keep back only the wound.

FIESCO (*shaken, rushes after her, stops her*). Leonora! What a scene! For God's sake!

LEONORA (*falls weakly into his arms*). I never deserved to become your wife, but your wife would have deserved to be respected. --How they whisper together now, the slanderers. How the ladies of Genoa and their daughters look askance at me. "See how she's losing her beauty, the little minx who married Fiesco." --Dreadful retribution for my woman's vainglory. I despised all my sex when Fiesco led me to the altar.

FIESCO. Now really, Madonna. This is a very odd scene.

LEONORA. There! He's turning white and turning red. Now I have courage.

FIESCO. Just two days, Countess, and you can pass judgment on me.

LEONORA. Sacrificed! --Let me not pronounce it in your hearing, virginal light! Sacrificed to a coquette. No! Look at me, my husband. But truly, the eyes that throw all Genoa into fits of abject trembling now must run and hide from the tears of a woman-

FIESCO (*very disconcerted*). No more, Signora. No further.

LEONORA (*sorrowful and somewhat bitter*). To flay a woman's frail heart. How worthy of the stronger sex! --I threw myself into the arms of this man. All my womanly weaknesses clasped this strong man in transports. I surrendered my whole heaven to him. And this magnanimous man gives it away to a--

FIESCO (*breaking in vehemently*). My Leonora, no!

LEONORA. My Leonora? --I thank you, Heaven. That was the authentic sound of love again. I ought to hate you, you traitor, and I throw myself starving on the crumbs of your affection. --Hate? Did I say *hate*, Fiesco? Oh, do not believe it. Your false oath can teach me to *die*, but never to hate. My heart has been deceived. (*Sound of the Moor approaching.*)

FIESCO. Leonora, grant me one small, childish request.

LEONORA. Anything, Fiesco, only not indifference.

FIESCO. What you like, as you like it-- (*Meaningful.*) Until Genoa is two days older, ask no questions. Make no condemnation. (*He conducts her becomingly into another room.*)

Scene 4

Moor, panting. Fiesco.

FIESCO. Why so out of breath?

MOOR. Quick, my Gracious Lord--

FIESCO. Something caught in our net?

MOOR. Read this letter! Am I really here? I think Genoa has grown twelve streets shorter, or my legs that much longer. You're turning white? Oh, yes. It seems it's heads they're drawing cards for and yours is the ace of spades. How does that agree with you?

FIESCO (*drops the letter on the table, shaken*). That curly head and ten devils! How did you get possession of this letter?

MOOR. About the same way--as Your Grace is getting possession of the Republic. A courier was supposed to gallop to Levanto with it. I smell fresh meat. Lie in ambush in a hollow way. Pow! The marten's done in--we have the hen.

FIESCO. His blood upon you! Gold wouldn't pay for this.

MOOR. Then I'll be content to have silver. (*Slowly and seriously.*) Count Lavagna. I had a hankering for your head lately. (*Pointing to the letter.*) Here's another. --Now, I should think, lout and Gracious Lord would be even. From now on you can address your thanks to a good friend. (*Hands him a second slip of paper.*) Number two.

FIESCO (*takes the sheet, astonished*). Are you out of your mind?

MOOR. Number two. (*He steps up beside him, impertinently, hands on hips.*) So the lion wasn't so dumb after all when he pardoned the mouse? (*Guileful.*) Right? He was a sly one. Who else would have gnawed him out of the net? --Well? How do you like *that*?

FIESCO. How many devils did you hire, fellow?

MOOR. At your service: only *one*, and he is in Your Honour's pay.

FIESCO. Doria's personal signature! --Where does this sheet come from?

MOOR. Fresh from the hands of my little Bononi.[51] I found my way to her last night, let her hear the ring of your fine words and of your even finer sequins. *They* got through to her. She told me to stop by again at six this morning. The Count really was there, like you said. And paid *black on white* his passage to a contraband kingdom of heaven.

FIESCO (*exasperated*). Those cheap skirt chasers! They want to bring down republics and can't keep the least thing from a bawd. I see here that Doria and company have plotted to murder me along with eleven Senators and to make Gianettino sovereign Duke.

MOOR. Quite right, and that on the morning when they elect a Doge, on the third of the month.

FIESCO (*rapidly*). Our nimble night is going to strangle that morrow in the womb. --Quick, Hassan. --My affairs are in readiness. --Call the others. --We want to be the first to draw. --Get moving, Hassan.

MOOR. I still have to unpack the rest of my news. Two thousand men have been successfully smuggled in. I've put them up at the Capuchins,' where no unmannerly sunbeam will find them out. They're wildly curious to see their new master and are fine fellows.

FIESCO. Out of every head will grow a scudo for you. What is Genoa muttering about my galleys?

MOOR. That's the best part, my Gracious Lord. Over four hundred soldiers of fortune, left stranded by the peace between France and Spain,[52] took up with my men and clamoured for a good word with you, so that you would send them against the Infidels. I told them to come into your courtyard at evening.

FIESCO (*pleased*). A bit more of this and I'll throw my arms around you, you rascal. Masterly! Four hundred, you say? --Genoa is beyond help. And you have four hundred scudi.

MOOR (*with simplicity*). What do you say, Fiesco? We two want to smash up Genoa until they can sweep up the laws with a broom. --What I've never told you: I have little birdies out in the local garrison, men I can count on like my descent into Hell. I've set it up so that we have at least six of ours among the watch at every gate, enough to talk up the others and put their five senses under a fog of wine. If you're inclined to mount something tonight, you'll find all the watches dead drunk.

FIESCO. Don't say another word. Up until now, I've shoved this huge block of granite along without human help, and here at the end the worst rascal in the territory should outdo me? Give me your hand, fellow. What the Count still owes you the Duke will make good.

MOOR. And in addition, a little note from the Countess Imperiali. She signalled me to come up from the lane, was very gracious, asked me as a joke if the Countess Lavagna hadn't had a touch of jaundice. Her Grace, said I, is inquiring after only *one* state of health--

FIESCO (*has read the note and tosses it aside*). Well said. And she answered?

MOOR. Answered that she nonetheless regretted the fate of the poor widow, that she would happily give her satisfaction and refuse Your Lordship's attentions in future.

FIESCO (*drily*). Which were going to cease before the arrival of the Millennium in any event. --Is *that* the extent of important matters, Hassan?

MOOR (*wickedly*). My Gracious Lord, ladies' affairs rank right behind political ones.

FIESCO. Yes, indeed, and certainly *these*. But what are you doing with that scrap of paper?

MOOR. I'm about to cancel one piece of devilry with another. Signora gave me these powders to stir one into your wife's chocolate every day.

FIESCO (*steps back, blanching*). Gave you?

MOOR. Donna Julia, Countess Imperiali.

FIESCO (*snatches them from him; fiercely*). If you are lying, you dog, I'll have you fixed live to the weathercock atop San Lorenzo, where *one* gust of wind will spin you around nine times. --These powders?

MOOR (*impatient*). I'm to give your wife to drink in her chocolate. On orders of Donna Julia Imperiali.

FIESCO (*beside himself*). Monstrous! Monstrous! --That lovely creature? --Can so much hell find room in the soul of one woman? --But I've forgotten to thank you, Divine Providence, for voiding it. --Voiding it by an even worse devil. Yours are mysterious ways. (*To the Moor.*) You are to promise to obey and to keep silent.

MOOR. Very well. The latter is easy: she paid for it in cash.

FIESCO. This note invites me to her. I shall come, Madame. I'll talk you around until you come here. Good, then. You move as fast as you can. Call the whole conspiracy together here.

MOOR. I saw this order coming, and on my own responsibility I've summoned every one of them for the stroke of ten.

FIESCO. I hear footsteps. It's them. Fellow, you would deserve your own gallows, where no son of Adam has ever swung before. Wait in the antechamber until I ring.

MOOR (*leaving*). The Moor has done his job, the Moor can go. (*Exit.*)

Scene 5

All Conspirators.

FIESCO (*advancing toward them*). The storm is gathering. The clouds are lowering. Step softly. Double-lock the door.

VERRINA. I have barred eight rooms after us. Suspicion can't come within a hundred paces.

BOURGOGNINO. There is no traitor here, unless it be our own fear.

FIESCO. Fear cannot cross my threshold. Welcome, all who are as you were yesterday. Take a seat. (*They sit down.*)

BOUGOGNINO (*walking about the room*). I don't like to sit when I'm contemplating overthrow.

FIESCO. Men of Genoa, this is a remarkable hour.

VERRINA. You charged us to reflect on a plan for tyrannicide. Poll us. We've come to give an account.

FIESCO. To begin with--a question that comes late enough to sound strange: *Who* shall fall?

(*All remain silent.*)

BOURGOGNINO (*leaning over Fiesco's chair; with meaning*). The tyrant*s*.

FIESCO. Well said, the tyrant*s*. I bid you consider the full weight of that word. One who *is on the point* of abolishing freedom, or one who has power to do so? Who is *more* the tyrant?

VERRINA. I hate the former, but the latter I fear. Andrea Doria must fall!

CALCAGNO (*moved*). Andrea, tired old Andrea, whose account with Nature may have fallen due day after tomorrow?

SACCO. Andrea, that mild-tempered old man?

FIESCO. This old man's mild temper is *fearsome*, dear Sacco; Gianettino's mad defiance is *laughable*. Andrea Doria must fall. Your good counsel tells us that, Verrina.

BOURGOGNINO. Chains of steel, chains of silk--they are no less chains, and Andrea Doria must fall.

FIESCO (*going to the table*). The staff broken over uncle and nephew, therefore! Give your signatures! (*All sign.*) We have decided *Who*. (*They sit down again.*) Now to the equally important *How*. --You speak first, friend Calcagno.

CALCAGNO. We can execute it like *soldiers* or like assassins. The first is *dangerous* because it forces us to have many accomplices and *rash* because the hearts of the nation are not yet fully won over. --For the *latter*, five good daggers will suffice. In three days a High Mass will be celebrated at San Lorenzo. Both Dorias worship there. Before the Almighty even tyrants lower their guard. I have spoken.

FIESCO (*has turned away*). Calcagno--your very reasonable opinion is atrocious. --Raffaele Sacco?

SACCO. I like Calcagno's reasons, but his proposal is an outrage. Better for Fiesco to have uncle and nephew invited to a dinner where they, hedged in by all the ill-will of the Republic, are made to choose: either eat death on our daggers or salute it with fine Cyprian wine. At least this method is convenient.

FIESCO (*horrified*). And if that drop of wine, on their dying tongues, becomes boiling pitch, the first taste of Hell? What *then*, Sacco? --Enough of such advice. You speak, Verrina.

VERRINA. An open heart presents an open countenance. A stealthy murder brings us into brotherhood with every bandit. A sword in the hand is the sign of the hero. My opinion is that we should sound the signal for insurrection and summon Genoa's patriots to avenge themselves by storm. (*He leaps up. The others follow. Bourgognino throws his arms around him.*)

BOURGOGNINO. And, sword in hand, force Fortune to favor us? That is the voice of honour, and it is my own.

FIESCO. And mine. (*To Calcagno and Sacco.*) Fie, Genoese. Fortune has already done too much for us; we must now do something for ourselves. --Insurrection, then, and *this very night*, men of Genoa! (*Verrina, Borgognino are astonished, the others frightened.*)

CALCAGNO. What? Tonight yet? The tyrants are still too powerful and our following still too thin.

SACCO. Tonight yet, and nothing has been done and the sun is already going down?

FIESCO. Your reservations are well founded. But read this. (*He hands them Gianettino's handwritten notes and walks up and down in malicious expectation as they read eagerly.*) Farewell now, Doria, bright star. Proud and impertinent, you stood there as if you had leased Genoa's whole horizon, and yet you saw that even the sun vacates the heavens and shares the world's scepter with the moon. Farewell, Doria, bright star.
        Patroclus, too, had to die,
        And was a better man than thou.[53]

BOURGOGNINO (*has read the writings*). This is horrible!

CALCAGNO. Twelve at one shot!

VERRINA. Tomorrow in the Signoria!

BOURGOGNINO. Give me those sheets. I'll ride straight through Genoa, holding them *so*, and the cobblestones behind me will explode and the dogs howl bloody murder.

ALL. Revenge! Revenge! Revenge! This very night!

FIESCO. Now you are where I wanted to have you. As soon as evening comes, I'll invite the most eminent malcontents to an entertainment: every name on Gianettino's hit list, and, in addition, the Sauli, Gentili, Vivaldi, and Vesodimari,[54] all mortal enemies of the house of Doria, whom that assassin forgot to live in fear of. They'll embrace my attempt on him with open arms, I do not doubt.

BOURGOGNINO. I do not doubt.

FIESCO. First and foremost, we must secure the *sea*. I have galleys and crews. The Dorias' twenty ships are unequipped, unmanned, easily surprised. The mouth of the Darsena is to be blockaded. All hope of flight bottled up. Once we have the harbour, Genoa is chained.

VERRINA. Undeniably.

FIESCO. Then we'll take and occupy the municipal strongholds. The most important is the St. Thomas Gate[55] toward the harbour, which communicates between our sea force and our land army. Both Dorias are to be surprised in their palaces and murdered. Alarm is to be struck in all the streets, the storm bells tolled. And the citizens called out to take up our cause and fight for Genoa's freedom. If Fortune favours us, you'll learn the rest in the Signoria.

VERRINA. The plan is good. Tell us how we divide the roles.

FIESCO (*with meaning*). Genoese, of your own volition you have put me at the head of this plot. Will you also obey my further orders?

VERRINA. As certainly as they are the best orders.

FIESCO. Verrina, do you know the motto posted beneath the flag? Tell him, men of Genoa: it says, *Subordination*! If I cannot turn these heads just as I want to-- Understand me well. If I am not sovereign in this conspiracy, it has lost one of its members.

VERRINA. A life of freedom is worth a few hours of servitude. --We shall obey.

FIESCO. Then leave me now. One of you will make the rounds of the city and report to me on the strength and weakness of the strongholds. Another will discover the password. A third will man the galleys. A fourth will bring the two thousand troops into my courtyard. I shall have put everything in order by evening and, in addition, as luck will have it, break the bank at faro. On the stroke of nine, everybody in the palace to receive my last orders. (*Rings.*)

VERRINA. I'll assume responsibility for the harbour. (*Exit.*)

BOURGOGNINO. I for the soldiers. (*Exit.*)

CALCAGNO. I'll find out the password. (*Exit.*)

SACCO. I'll make the rounds of Genoa. (*Exit.*)

Scene 6

Fiesco. Then the Moor.

FIESCO (*has seated himself at a desk and is writing*). Didn't they recoil at the word *subordination*, like a caterpillar pricked by a needle? --Too late now, Republicans.

MOOR (*entering*). Gracious Lord--

FIESCO (*stands up, gives him a sheet of paper*). All whose names appear here are to be invited to a *comedy* tonight.

MOOR. To take part in it, presumably. Admittance at the price of your head.

FIESCO (*distant and contemptuous*). When that's attended to, I'll not delay you here in Genoa any longer. (*He leaves the room, letting a purse fall behind him.*) That will be your last task. (*Exit.*)

Scene 7

The Moor slowly picks up the purse, gazing after Fiesco in surprise.

MOOR. Is that how we stand? *I'll not delay you here in Genoa any longer.* Translated from the Christian into my Heathen, it says: *When I'm Duke, I'll have my good friend hanged on a Genoese gallows.* Fine. He's afraid that I, knowing his little ways, will make his honour hostage to my big mouth, once he's Duke. Careful, my Lord Count. That might be worth considering. And now, old Doria, I dispose over your hide. --You're *done* if I don't warn you. If I go there now and denounce the plot, I'll have rescued nothing less than the life and the duchy of the Duke of Genoa; nothing less than this hat brim-full of gold can be his thanks. (*He is about to go, then stops abruptly.*) Not so fast, friend Hassan. Are you on your way to doing something stupid? --If the whole massacre didn't happen and something *good* came of it? --Pooh! Pooh! What kind of dirty trick is my greed playing on me! --What makes for more trouble? If I do in Fiesco here? --Or if I deliver Doria there to the knife? --You figure it out, devils of mine. --If Fiesco brings it off, Genoa can rise. Rubbish! That can't be. If this Doria wriggles through, everything stays the same, and Genoa will have peace. --That's even more disgusting! --But what a spectacle, when the heads of the rebels go flying into the hangman's chophouse! (*Crossing to the other side.*) But all that jolly butchery tonight when Their Graces choke to death on the smarts of a Moor! Ugh! We'll let a Christian find his way out of this tangle; the riddle is too thorny for a heathen. --I want to consult an expert. (*Exit.*)

Scene 8

Salon of the Countess Imperiali. Julia en négligé. Gianettino enters in disarray.

GIANETTINO. Good evening, Sister.

JULIA (*stands up*). It would be something extraordinary that brings the Crown Prince of Genoa to his sister?

GIANETTINO. Sister, you are swarmed about by butterflies, I by wasps. Who can find time to get away? Let's sit down.

JULIA. I'm going to lose patience with you.

GIANETTINO. Sister, when did Fiesco last visit you?

JULIA. Odd. As if I made a note of such bagatelles.

GIANETTINO. I really have to know.

JULIA. Fine. He came by yesterday.

GIANETTINO. And seemed *at ease?*

JULIA. As usual.

GIANETTINO. Still the same old *fantast*?

JULIA (*insulted*). Brother!

GIANETTINO (*raising his voice*). Hear me! Still the same old fantast?

JULIA (*stands up, angered*). What do you take me for, Brother?

GIANETTINO (*remains seated; with malice*). For a piece of female flesh wrapped up in a great big patent of nobility. Between us, Sister, since no one's listening in.

JULIA (*hotly*). Between us--you are a hot-headed jackanapes mounted on your uncle's credit as if it were a hobbyhorse. --Since no one's listening in.

GIANETTINO. Sisterkins! Sisterkins! Temper! Temper! --I'm just amused that Fiesco is still the same old fantast. That's what I wanted to know. Compliments. (*About to leave.*)

Scene 9

Lomellino enters.

LOMELLINO (*kisses Julia's hand*). Forgive the intrusion, my Gracious Lady. (*Turned toward Gianettino.*) Certain things that suffer no delay--

GIANETTINO (*takes him aside. Julia goes angrily to a piano and plays an allegro*). Everything ready for tomorrow?

LOMELLINO. Everything, Prince. But the courier who raced off to Levanto this morning has not returned. And Spinola hasn't come. If he's been picked up? --I'm very uneasy.

GIANETTINO. Nothing to worry about. You've kept the list on your person?

LOMELLINO (*awkward*). My Gracious Lord--the list--I'm not sure--it's probably in the coat I wore yesterday--

GIANETTINO. Fine. If only Spinola had arrived. Fiesco will be found dead in his bed tomorrow morning. I've made arrangements.

LOMELLINO. It's going to create a terrible stir.

GIANETTINO. That precisely is our safety, boy. Everyday offences inflame the blood of the victim, and the man is capable of anything.

Extraordinary crimes freeze the blood, and he's nothing. Do you know the tale about the head of the Medusa? The sight turns you to *stone*. And what one can't get done before stone warms up again!

LOMELLINO. Have you said anything to the Lady?

GIANETTINO. Certainly not! One has to be careful with her on the subject of Fiesco. But when she's once tasted the fruit, she'll not make a fuss about the price. Come. I'm expecting troops from Milan this evening and must leave orders at the gates. (*To Julia.*) Well, Sister? Will it take you much longer to bang away your anger?

JULIA. Go. You're an unmannerly guest.

(*Gianettino, leaving, bumps into Fiesco.*)

Scene 10

Fiesco enters.

GIANETTINO (*starting back*). Ha!

FIESCO (*obliging, engaging*). Prince, you spare me a visit that I was intending--

GIANETTINO. I, too, Count, could meet with nothing more desirable than your society.

FIESCO (*goes to Julia and kisses her hand respectfully*). And in your company, Signora, one is accustomed to always seeing one's expectations exceeded.

JULIA. Tut, tut. That would sound ambiguous said to someone else. But I'm appalled at my *négligé*. Excuse me, Count. (*About to retreat into her dressing room.*)

FIESCO. Oh, stay, lovely Gracious Lady. Womankind is at its loveliest when attired for the night, (*smiling*) it's the costume of the trade. --Your piled-up hair--let me muss it up entirely.

JULIA. How you men like to muss things up!

FIESCO (*innocently, to Gianettino*). Hair and republics: it's all the same to us, isn't it? --This ribbon has also been tacked on wrong. --Have a seat, lovely Countess. --Your Laura knows how to deceive our eyes, but not our hearts. --Let me be your chambermaid. (*She sits down; he adjusts her garment.*)

GIANETTINO (*tugs Lomellino's sleeve*). He doesn't suspect a thing, poor devil.

FIESCO (*busy at Julia's bosom*). You see? I'm concealing *this* for good reason. The senses must carry their message blind, not knowing how Nature and Fantasy have arranged the game.

JULIA. That's frivolous.

FIESCO. Not at all. For, you know, the best of late-breaking news loses something when it becomes the talk of the town. --Our senses are only the basic broth of our inner republic. The nobility lives on them but raises itself above the flatness of their taste. (*He has readied her and leads her before a mirror.*) Upon my honour! Tomorrow this outfit must become Genoa's latest fashion. (*With fineness.*) May I conduct you through town like this, Countess?

JULIA. What a sly-boots! How artfully he's arranged to flatter me into getting his way. But I have a headache and shall remain at home.

FIESCO. Forgive me, Countess--you may do as you like, but that you do not like. --This noon a troupe of Florentine players arrived in town and has offered to play in my palace. --Now, I was not able to hinder that the greater part of our noblewomen will want to attend the spectacle. This is a source of embarrassment, for I don't know how to fill the box of honour without offending my susceptible guests. There is but *one* escape (*bowing deeply*): Would you be so gracious, Signora?

JULIA (*changes colour and goes straight into her dressing room*). Laura!

GIANETTINO (*approaches Fiesco*). Count, you may remember an unpleasant affair that took place between us recently--

FIESCO. I would wish, Prince, that we should both forget it. --We men treat one another in keeping with our knowledge, and whose fault is it but mine that my friend Doria knew me but badly?

GIANETTINO. In any case, I shall never think of it without sincerely asking your forgiveness--

FIESCO. Nor I without sincerely forgiving you. (*Julia returns, her costume somewhat altered.*)

GIANETTINO. --It just occurs to me, Count: You're sending ships against the Turks?

FIESCO. They weigh anchor this evening. --And I have some concerns here, from which the kindness of my friend Doria could deliver me.

GIANETTINO (*very polite*). With the greatest pleasure! --Dispose over all my influence.

FIESCO. Events toward evening might draw a crowd toward the harbour and before my palace that the Duke, your uncle, could misinterpret--

GIANETTINO (*heartily*). Let that be *my* concern. Carry on, and I wish you good fortune in your undertaking.

FIESCO (*smiles*). I'm very much obliged to you.

Scene 11

As above. A German from the bodyguard.

GIANETTINO (*testy*). Yes?

GERMAN. As I was passing the St. Thomas Gate, I saw a large number of armed soldiers hurrying toward the Darsena and rigging Count Lavagna's galleys for sailing--

GIANETTINO. Nothing more important? Not to be passed on.

GERMAN. Very well. There's also a suspicious-looking rabble pouring out of the Capuchin cloisters and stealing across the market. Their looks and the way they walk suggest that they are soldiers.

GIANETTINO (*angry*). The officiousness of an idiot! (*To Lomellino, confidently.*) Those are my Milanese.

GERMAN. Does Your Grace order that they be arrested?

GIANETTINO (*aloud to Lomellino*). Look into it, Lomellino. (*Furious, to the German.*) Go! That's enough. (*To Lomellino.*) Make plain to that German ox that he's to keep his mouth shut. (*Exit Lomellino with the German.*)

FIESCO (*who has been flirting with Julia meanwhile and casting stolen glances at the others*). Our friend is irritated. May I know the reason?

GIANETTINO. No wonder. All this eternal inquire-and-report-back. (*Goes shooting out.*)

FIESCO. The spectacle awaits us, too. May I offer you my arm, my Gracious Lady?

JULIA. Patience. I must first throw my wrapper around me. But no tragedy, Count. It'll come back to me in dreams.

FIESCO (*mischievous*). Oh, you'll die laughing, Countess. (*He leads her off.*)

(*Curtain.*)

Act Four

It is night. Courtyard of Fiesco's palace. The lanterns are being lit, weapons are being brought in. One wing of the palace is illuminated.

Scene 1

Bourgognino leads in Soldiers.

BOUGOGNINO. Halt! --Four sentries to the main courtyard gate. Two to each entrance to the palace. (*Guards take their posts.*) Anyone who wishes to enter will be admitted. No one may leave again. Any use of force will be struck down. (*Takes the rest of the troops into the palace. Sentries walk up and down. Pause.*)

Scene 2

SENTRIES AT COURTYARD GATE (*call out*). Who goes there? (*Centurione enters.*)

CENTURIONE. Friend of Lavagna. (*Crosses the courtyard toward the entrance on the right.*)

SENTRIES (*there*). Stand back.

CENTURIONE (*stops short, then crosses toward the left entrance*).

SENTRIES (*on left*). Stand back.

CENTURIONE (*stands still, baffled. Pause. Then to the Watch on the left*). Friend? Which way to the play?

SENTRY. Can't say.

CENTURIONE (*walks up and down in growing bafflement, then to the Watch on the right*). Friend, when does the play begin?

SENTRY. Can't say.

CENTURIONE (*astonished. Walks up and down. Starts at the sight of the weapons*). Friend? What's this for?

SENTRY. Can't say.

CENTURIONE (*wraps his cloak around himself, very uneasy*). Strange!

SENTRIES AT COURTYARD GATE (*call out*). Who goes there?

Scene 3

As above. Cibo enters.

CIBO (*entering*). Friend of Lavagna.

CENTURIONE. Cibo, where do we find ourselves?

CIBO. What?

CENTURIONE. Look around, Cibo.

CIBO. Where? What?

CENTURIONE. All the entrances guarded.

CIBO. There are weapons lying here.

CENTURIONE. No one will explain.

CIBO. That's curious.

CENTURIONE. What's the hour?

CIBO. After eight.

CENTURIONE. Foo! It's bitter cold.

CIBO. Eight is the appointed hour.

CENTURIONE (*shaking his head*). There's something wrong here.

CIBO. Fiesco's planning some joke.

CENTURIONE. Tomorrow we elect a Doge. --Cibo, something's wrong here.

CIBO. Shh! Shh! Shh!

CENTURIONE. The right wing is full of lights.

CIBO. Don't you hear something? Don't you hear something?

CENTURIONE. A low murmuring in there and now and then--

CIBO. A muffled rattling, as if of armour rubbing together--

CENTURIONE. Horrible! Horrible!

CIBO. A carriage! It's stopping at the gate!

SENTRIES AT COURTYARD GATE (*call out*). Who goes there?

Scene 4

As above. The four Asserati.

ASSERATO (*entering*). Friend of Fiesco.

CIBO. It's the four Asserati.

CENTURIONE. Good evening, countryman.

ASSERATO. We're going to the play.

CIBO. Good luck to you.

ASSERATO. Aren't you also going to the play?

CENTURIONE. Please go first. We want to catch a breath of fresh air.

ASSERATO. It starts soon. Come. (*They go forward.*)

SENTRY. Stand back!

ASSERATO. What's intended here?

CENTURIONE (*laughs*). Try tending toward the palace.

ASSERATO. There's some misunderstanding.

CIBO. Manifestly. (*Music in the right wing.*)

ASSERATO. Do you hear the concert? The comedy seems to be about to begin.

CENTURIONE. It seems to *me* it's already begun, and we're playing the fools in it.

CIBO. I'm not all that wild about it anymore. I'm leaving.

ASSERATO. Weapons, yet!

CIBO. Pooh! Stage props.

CENTURIONE. Are we supposed to stand here like fools on the banks of Acheron?[56] Come! Off to the coffee house! (*All six hurry toward the gate.*)

SENTRIES (*cry loudly*). Stand back!

CENTURIONE. Death and destruction! We're prisoners!

CIBO. My sword says: Not for long.

ASSERATO. Put up! Put up! The Count is a man of honour.

CIBO. Sold out! Betrayed! That play was bait, and the trap has slammed shut behind the mouse.

ASSERATO. God forbid! I dread to know what will come of this.

Scene 5

SENTRIES. Who goes there? (*Verrina, Sacco enter.*)

VERRINA. Friends of the house. (*Seven other Noblemen follow.*)

CIBO. His intimates! Now we'll get some clarity.

SACCO (*in conversation with Verrina*). As I told you, Lescaro[57] has the watch at the St. Thomas Gate. Doria's best officer and blindly loyal to him.

VERRINA. That's good.

CIBO (*to Verrina*). You come just in time to help us all out of a dream.

VERRINA. How so? How so?

CENTURIONE. We've been invited to a play.

VERRINA. Then we're going the same way.

CENTURIONE (*impatient*). The way of all flesh. *That* one I'm acquainted with. You surely see that the entrances are guarded? Why guard the entrances?

CIBO. Why the weapons?

CENTURIONE. We're standing around as if under the gallows.

VERRINA. The Count himself is coming.

CENTURIONE. Let him be quick about it. My patience is running out. (*All Noblemen walk up and down in the background.*)

BOURGOGNINO (*from the palace*). What news from the harbour, Verrina?

VERRINA. Everybody safely on board.

BOURGOGNINO. The palace is also stuffed full of soldiers.

VERRINA. It's nearly nine o'clock.

BOURGOGNINO. The Count is slow.

VERRINA. But still too speedy for his hopes. Bougognino, my blood freezes when I think--

BOURGOGNINO. Nothing in haste, Father.

VERRINA. There's no being *hasty* when there can be no *delay*. If I can't commit the second murder, I'll never justify the first.

BOURGOGNINO. But *when* is Fiesco to die?

VERRINA. When Genoa is free, Fiesco dies.

SENTRIES. Who goes there?

Scene 6

As above. Fiesco.

FIESCO (*entering*). A friend. (*All bow. The Sentries present arms.*) Welcome, my worthy guests. You will have complained of your host's tardiness. I apologize. (*Softly to Verrina.*) All done?

VERRINA (*to his ear*). Perfectly.

FIESCO (*softly to Bourgognino*). And?

BOURGOGNINO. Everything in order.

FIESCO (*to Sacco*). And?

SACCO. All's well.

FIESCO. And Calcagno?

BOURGOGNINO. Not back yet.

FIESCO (*aloud to the Watch at the gate*). Gates closed. (*He takes off his hat and approaches the gathered Company with easy presence.*) My Lords! I took the liberty of inviting you to a play. Not, however, for your entertainment, but to give you a role in it. My friends, we have endured Gianettino Doria's defiance and Andrea's presumptuousness long enough. If we want to save Genoa, friends, we have no time to lose. To what end, think you, the twenty galleys that occupy our country's harbour? To what end such alliances as these Dorias have concluded? To what end the foreign arms they have brought into the heart of Genoa? --Grumbling and cursing are now no longer enough. To save *all* we must dare *all*. A desperate evil requires a bold remedy. Can there be anyone present in this company so phlegmatic as to acknowledge a master who is no more than his equal? --(*Murmuring.*)-- There is not one among us whose ancestors did not stand around Genoa's cradle. What, then, by all that is sacred, what excellence do those two citizens enjoy that they should impertinently take flight over our heads? --(*More agitated grumbling.*)-- Each of you is solemnly called upon to defend Genoa's cause against its oppressors. --Not one among you can forfeit a hair's breadth of *his* rights without thereby betraying the soul of the entire State--

(*Agitation among his hearers interrupts him. Then he continues.*)

You feel-- Everything has been gained now. I have already opened the way to glory before you. Will you follow? I am ready to lead you. These preparations--that you have but fleetingly regarded and with horror--these preparations must inspire a renewed spirit of heroism in you. Those shudders of alarm must take on warmth and become a glorious eagerness to make common cause with these patriots and with me, and to bring these tyrants down resoundingly. Success will favour our daring, for my preparations are good. Our undertaking is just, for Genoa is suffering. The intention makes us immortal, for it is dangerous and tremendous.

CENTURIONE (*in a stormy burst of feeling*). Enough! Genoa will be free! With this battle cry, against the gates of Hell.

CIBO. Anyone whom that does not rouse from his slumber--may he pant at his oar until the trumpets of the Last Judgment sound to release him.

FIESCO. Those were the words of a man. Now you deserve to know the danger that has hung over you and Genoa. (*He gives them the papers that the Moor produced.*) Light here, soldiers! (*The Noblemen crowd around a torch and read.*) That's the effect I wanted, friend.

VERRINA. Not so loud. There on the left I saw faces go pale and knees knock together.

CENTURIONE (*enraged*). Twelve Senators! Fiendish! Everybody take up a sword. (*All but two fall upon the ready weapons.*)

CIBO. Your name's there, too, Bourgognino.

BOURGOGNINO. And today yet on Doria's throat, God willing.

CENTURIONE. Two swords are still lying there.

CIBO. What? What?

CENTURIONE. Two did not pick up a sword.

ASSERATO. My brothers cannot bear the sight of blood. Spare them.

CENTURIONE (*remonstrating*). What? What? The sight of a tyrant's blood? Skin the mollies. Throw them out of the Republic, the bastards. (*Some of the Company angrily attack the two.*)

FIESCO (*separating them*). Halt! Halt! Is Genoa to owe its freedom to slaves? Should our gold, alloyed with base metal, lose its ring of authenticity? (*He frees them.*) You, gentlemen, will content yourselves with a chamber in my palace until our affairs have been decided. (*To the Watch.*) Two prisoners. You will answer for them. Two armed sentries on their threshold. (*They are led away.*)

WATCH AT THE COURTYARD GATE. Who goes there? (*Knocking.*)

CALCAGNO (*calls in fright*). Open up! A friend! For God's sake, open up.

BOURGOGNINO. It's Calcagno. What's this "for God's sake"?

FIESCO. Open for him, soldiers.

Scene 7

As above. Calcagno enters, breathless, frightened.

CALCAGNO. Done for. Done for. Run for your lives. It's all over.

BOURGOGNINO. What's *over*? Do they have flesh of cast iron?[58] Are our swords reeds?

FIESCO. Steady, Calcagno! A misunderstanding here would be unforgivable.

CALCAGNO. We've been betrayed. A hellish truth. Your Moor, Lavagna, the rascal. I've just come from the palace of the Signoria. He had an audience with the Duke. (*All the Noblemen go pale; even Fiesco changes colour.*)

VERRINA (*resolutely to the Watch at the gate*). Soldiers, extend your halberds. I shall not die at the hands of the hangman. (*The Noblemen rush about in consternation.*)

FIESCO (*more resolute*). Where are you going? What are you doing? --The devil take you, Calcagno. --It was a false alarm, gentlemen. --Hysterical woman! To say such a thing before these schoolboys. --You, too, Verrina? --Bourgognino, you, too? --Where are you going?

BOURGOGNINO (*brutal*). Home! To murder my Berta and then come back here.

FIESCO (*bursts out laughing*). Stay! Stop! Is that the courage of tyrannicides? --Masterful acting, Calcagno. --Did nobody notice that this news was of *my* making? --Calcagno, speak. Wasn't it *my* order to put these Romans to the test?

VERRINA. Well, if you can laugh? --I'll credit it, or never think you human again.

FIESCO. Shame on you men. To fail a schoolboy's test. --Pick up your weapons. --You'll have to fight like bears to make good this loss of nerve. (*Softly to Calcagno.*) Were you yourself present?

CALCAGNO. I pushed my way through the bodyguards to get the password from the Duke, as ordered. --I'm about to leave when they bring in the Moor.

FIESCO (*aloud*). So the old man has gone to bed? We'll flush him out of there. (*Softly.*) Did he have a long conversation with the Duke?

CALCAGNO. I was so startled and you in such danger that I hardly stayed two minutes.

FIESCO (*loud and cheerful*). Look how our countrymen still quake.

CALCAGNO. They shouldn't have gone to pieces so easily. (*Softly.*) But for God's sake, Count! What's the good of all these lies?

FIESCO. *Time*, friend, until the first shock has passed. (*Aloud.*) Hey! Bring us wine. (*Softly.*) Did you see the Duke turn pale? (*Aloud.*) Chin up, brothers! We want to toast the evening's dancing! (*Softly.*) Did you see the Duke turn pale?

CALCAGNO. The Moor's first word must have been *conspiracy*. The old man started back, white as a sheet.

FIESCO (*bewildered*). Hm! Hm! He's a sly devil, Calcagno. He betrayed nothing until they had the knife against their throats. Now he's their darling. The Moor is sly. (*A Servant brings a cup of wine; he holds it up to the Company and drinks.*) To our good fortune, comrades! (*Knocking at the gate.*)

SENTRIES. Who's there?

A VOICE. Orderlies of the Duke. (*The Noblemen rush around the courtyard in despair.*)

FIESCO (*intervening*). No, friends, no! Don't be frightened! Don't be frightened! *I* am here. Quick! Get rid of these weapons. Be men, I beg you. This visit gives me hope that Andrea still has doubts. Go inside. Compose yourselves. -- Open, soldiers. (*All withdraw; the gate is opened.*)

Scene 8

Fiesco, as if coming from the palace. Three Germans, who bring in the Moor, bound.

FIESCO. Who called me into the courtyard?

GERMAN. Bring us to the Count.

FIESCO. The Count is here. Who asks for me?

GERMAN (*performs honours*). The Duke wishes you good evening. He sends Your Honour this Moor, bound, who, he bids me report, has prattled shamefully. His note will tell you the rest.

FIESCO (*takes the Moor with indifference*). And didn't I promise you the galleys this very day? (*To the German.*) Very good, friend. My respects to the Duke.

MOOR (*calls after them*). Respects from me, too. And tell him--the Duke--if he hadn't sent a jackass, he would have found out that two thousand soldiers have been tucked into that palace. (*The Germans leave. The Noblemen return.*)

Scene 9

Fiesco, Conspirators. The Moor defiantly in their midst.

CONSPIRATORS (*starting back fearfully at the sight of the Moor*). Ha! What is this?

FIESCO (*has read the note; with suppressed rage*). Men of Genoa! The danger has passed. --And so has the conspiracy.

VERRINA (*calls out, astonished*). What? Are the Dorias dead?

FIESCO (*much aroused*). By God! The whole military might of the Republic-- *that* I was prepared for. But not for this. In four lines that feeble old man defeats fifteen hundred men. (*Drops his arms.*) Doria defeats Fiesco.

BOURGOGNINO. Explain, would you? We're rooted to the spot.

FIESCO (*reads*). "Lavagna, it seems you have quite a fate with me: You reap thanklessness for your good deeds. This Moor warns me of a plot. --I return him to you, bound, and shall sleep tonight *without bodyguard*." (*He lets the note fall. They all look at one another.*)

VERRINA. Well, Fiesco?

FIESCO (*nobly*). A Doria should exceed me in magnanimity? There should be *one* virtue lacking in the pedigree of the Fieschi? --No! As sure as I am who I am! --Disperse, gentlemen. I shall go to him--and confess all. (*About to hurry out.*)

VERRINA (*stops him*). Are you out of your mind, you? Was it some kind of schoolboy's prank that we were planning? Stop! Or wasn't it the cause of our fatherland? Stop! Or was it only *Andrea* you wanted to attack, and not the tyrant? Stop, I say. --I arrest you as a traitor to the State--

CONSPIRATORS. Tie him up! Throw him to the ground!

FIESCO (*snatches a sword from someone and opens a path for himself*). Easy, now. Who'll be the first to throw a halter over the tiger? --Do you see, gentlemen? --I am free. --I could make my way through you if I wanted to. --But now I will stay; I've changed my mind.

BOURGOGNINO. Put your mind on your duty?

FIESCO (*angered, proudly*). Ho, my boy. You mind the duty that you owe *me* first, and watch your tongue. --At ease, gentlemen. --Nothing has changed. (*To the Moor, whose restraints he cuts.*) It is your desert *to have occasioned a great deed.* --Now flee!

CALCAGNO (*angry*). What? What? This heathen has betrayed all of us and yet lives?

FIESCO. Has *frightened* all of you and yet lives. Be gone, fellow! See to it that you put Genoa at your back, or they might use you to redeem their courage.

MOOR. So, the Devil never fails a rogue! Your servant, sirs. --I notice that my noose won't grow in Italy. I'll have to look for it elsewhere. (*Exit, laughing.*)

Scene 10

A Servant enters. As above, without the Moor.

SERVANT. The Countess Imperiali has asked for Your Honour three times.

FIESCO. I say! The play is going to have to start! Tell her I will be there immediately. --Stay! --You will ask my wife to come into the concert hall and to wait for me there behind the tapestries. (*Exit Servant.*) I've written out all your roles, how each one is to accomplish his, so there's nothing more to say. --Verrina will go ahead of us to the harbour. When he has captured the ships, he'll *give the signal for breaking out with cannon.* --I must go. I'm called away by a matter of importance. You will hear a bell and all come into my concert hall together. --Meanwhile, go in--and enjoy my Cyprian wine.

(*They disperse.*)

Scene 11

Concert hall. Leonora. Arabella. Rosa. All anxious.

LEONORA. Fiesco promised to come into the concert hall, and yet he doesn't come. It's after eleven. The palace rumbles dreadfully with weapons and men, and no Fiesco?

ROSA. You're to conceal yourself behind the tapestries. --What our Master could mean by that?

LEONORA. He wishes it, Rosa, and that is enough to command my obedience. Enough, Bella, not to be at all afraid. --But still, still I tremble so, Bella, and my heart pounds so fearfully. In God's name, girls, don't either of you leave my side.

BELLA. Don't be afraid of anything. Our anxiety has checked our impertinence.

LEONORA. Wherever I look, I meet strange faces, *hollow* and *distorted* like ghosts. Whoever I call to trembles like someone seized and flees into the deepest darkness, *this horrible hostel of bad conscience.* For answer I get a fleeting, inaudible sound that hesitates still on a quivering tongue, whether it dare slip clean away. --Fiesco? --I don't know what dreadful business is brewing here-- (*Folding her hands gracefully.*) Guard my Fiesco, Heavenly Host.

ROSE (*starting*). Jesus! What's that noise in the gallery?

BELLA. It's the soldier on guard there. (*The Sentry outside the door calls, "Who goes there?" There is an answer.*)

LEONORA. People are coming. Behind the tapestry! Quick! (*They conceal themselves.*)

Scene 12

Julia, Fiesco, in conversation.

JULIA (*very stirred up*). No more, Count. Your gallantries no longer fall on deaf ears but into my seething blood. --Where am I? There's no one here but the seductive night. Where have you led my desolated heart with your chatter?

FIESCO. Where balked passion becomes more bold, and transport speaks more freely to transport.

JULIA. Stop here, Fiesco. By all that is sacred, no farther. If this darkness were not so deep, you would see my flaming cheeks and relent.

FIESCO. Quite wrong, Julia. Then precisely *my* feeling would sense the fiery banner of your *own* and overflow with greater courage. (*He kisses her hand fervently.*)

JULIA. Why, your face burns as feverishly as your words. Alas, from my own--I feel it--a wild, wanton fire flames out. Let's go back to the light, I beg you. Our agitated senses could heed the dangerous call of these shadows. Oh, go. Those seething rebels could exercise their godless arts behind the back of blushing day. Return to the company, I entreat you!

FIESCO (*more pressing*). How concerned you are, and without cause, my dear! Is the mistress ever to be in fear her slave?

JULIA. Oh, you men and your eternal contradiction! As if you weren't the most dangerous of victors just when you surrender to our amour propre. Shall I confess all, Fiesco? That only my vice preserved my virtue? Only my pride mocked your arts? That my principles held only to this point? You despair of your devices and have recourse to Julia's blood. And here those principles desert me.

FIESCO (*frivolously bold*). And what did you lose by this loss?

JULIA (*excited and heatedly*). If I should squander the key to my woman's sanctuary on you, so that you can make me scarlet with shame, if you like? Have I less to lose then everything? Do you want to know more, you scoffer? Do you want me to confess that all the *secret wisdom* of our sex is only a wretched defence to *relieve* our mortal side, which in the end is only going to be *besieged* by your oaths; which (I confess it with shame) so much wants to be *conquered,* so often receives the enemy traitorously at the first inattentiveness of virtue? That all our womanly arts do battle solely for this defenceless prize, just as on the *chessboard* all the knights cover the defenceless king? If you take him by surprise-- checkmate! And you can safely toss the whole board over. (*After a pause, earnestly.*) You now have the picture of our resplendent poverty. --Be magnanimous.

FIESCO. And yet, Julia--where better to put down this treasure than in my endless passion?

JULIA. Nowhere better and nowhere worse, surely. --Tell me, Fiesco, how long will this endlessness last? --Oh, I have already played too unluckily not to wager all I have left. --Fiesco, I was bold enough to believe my charms would *catch* you, but I doubt they have the omnipotence to *hold* you. --Horrors! What am I saying? (*She steps back and covers her face with her hands.*)

FIESCO. Two sins in *one* breath. Mistrust of my taste or lèse-majesté of your own lovableness? --Which of the two is harder to forgive?

JULIA (*languid, surrendering, affecting*). Lies are but the weapons of Hell. --Fiesco no longer needs them to fell his Julia. (*She sinks exhausted onto a sofa; after a pause, solemnly.*) One little word, Fiesco-- Hear me: We are *heroines* when we know our virtue still *safe;* when we *defend* it, *children;* (*staring at him fixedly, wildly*) and *furies* when we *avenge* it. --Ah, Fiesco, what if you should strangle me cold?

FIESCO (*assuming an angry tone*). Cold? Cold? --By God, what the unappeasable vanity of woman doesn't demand, when she sees a *man* grovel before her and still has doubts! Ha! He's waking up again, I feel it. (*Changes to a cold tone.*) My eyes have been opened in good time. --What was it I was just begging for? On the highest favour of a woman the least humiliation of a man is wholly thrown away! (*To her, with a deep, frosty bow.*) Take courage, Madame. You are now entirely safe.

JULIA (*startled*). Count? What's come over you?

FIESCO (*wholly indifferent*). No, Madame. You're quite right, we two see our honour in play only *once.* (*Kisses her hand politely.*) It is my pleasure to show you my respects before the company. (*About to leave quickly.*)

JULIA (*after him, pulls him back*). Stay! Are you mad? Stay! Must I say--confess--what the whole male tribe, on its knees--in tears--on the rack, would never have wrung from my pride? --Alas! Even this deep darkness is too bright to conceal the burning fire that this confession lays upon my cheeks. --Fiesco--oh, I pierce the heart of all my sex--all my sex will hate me forever--Fiesco, I adore you. (*She falls down before him.*)

FIESCO (*retreats three steps, lets her lie, and laughs triumphantly*). I regret that, Signora. (*He pulls the bell, raises the tapestry, and leads out Leonora.*) Here is my wife--a god-like woman. (*He embraces Leonora.*)

JULIA (*leaps up, crying*). Oh! Outrageously deceived!

Scene 13

The Conspirators, who enter together. Ladies from the opposite side. Fiesco. Leonora and Julia.

LEONORA. My husband, that was far too severe.

FIESCO. A wicked heart deserved no less. I owed *your* tears this satisfaction. (*To the Company.*) No, ladies and gentlemen, it is not my habit to burst into flames at every provocation, like a child. The idiocies of men amuse me long before they begin to irritate me. But *this* creature deserves all my anger, for she has prepared this powder for this angel. (*He shows the poison to the Company, who draw back in horror.*)

JULIA (*swallowing her rage*). Good! Good! Very good, my Lord. (*Moves to leave.*)

FIESCO (*conducts her back again*). Patience, please, Madame. We are not yet done-- This company is all too eager to know why I could so gainsay my good sense as to enact a mad romance with Genoa's greatest fool--

JULIA (*leaping up*). Insupportable! Tremble, you. (*Threatening.*) Doria thunders in Genoa, and I--am his sister.

FIESCO. A great pity, if this is your *last* burst of *gall*. --I regret to inform you that Fiesco di Lavagna has turned the stolen diadem of His Grace your brother into a rope with which he is disposed to string up that thief of the Republic tonight. (*She blanches, and he laughs maliciously.*) Hoo! That was unexpected-- And, you see (*more biting as he continues*), *that's* why I found it necessary to give the importuning eyes of your household something to amuse them, *that's* why I decked myself out (*pointing at her*) in this Harlequin's passion, *that's* why (*indicating Leonora*) I abandoned this jewel. And, happily, my quarry ran straight into my spread nets. --I thank you for your kindness, Signora, and return my costume jewellery. (*He returns her silhouette to her with a bow.*)

LEONORA (*folds herself into his arms, pleading*). My Ludovico, she's *weeping*. May your Leonora beg you, trembling?

JULIA (*haughtily, to Leonora*). Quiet, you hateful--

FIESCO (*to a Servant*). Be so gallant, friend-- Offer this lady your arm. She wishes to visit my state prison. You shall ensure that no one inconvenience Madonna. --There's a high wind outside. --The storm that splits the family tree of Doria tonight might--spoil her coiffure.

JULIA (*sobbing*). A pox upon you, you treacherous black deceiver. (*To Leonora, fiercely.*) You've not triumphed. He'll destroy *you*, too, and *himself*--and despair. (*Rushes out.*)

FIESCO (*signals his Guests*). You are my witnesses-- Restore my honour in Genoa! (*To the Conspirators.*) You will come for me when the cannon sounds. (*All withdraw.*)

Scene 14

Leonora. Fiesco.

LEONORA (*approaches him anxiously*). Fiesco? --Fiesco? --I only half understand you, but I begin to tremble.

FIESCO (*significantly*). Leonora-- I once saw you pass to the left side of a Genoese lady-- In the assemblies of the nobles, I saw you content yourself with the knights' kissing your hand second. Leonora--that offended my eyes. And I decided this shall be no more--it shall end. Do you hear the war-like rumblings in my palace? What you fear is true. --Go to bed, Countess. --Tomorrow I shall wake--the *Duchess*.

LEONORA (*clasps herself about the shoulders and throws herself into a chair*). Oh, my prophetic soul! I am lost!

FIESCO (*firmly, with dignity*). Let me finish, my love. Two of my ancestors wore the Triple Crown;[59] the blood of the Fieschi runs warm only under the Purple. Is your husband to reflect only inherited glory? (*More vivid.*) What? Is he to attribute all his stature to fickle Fortune, which, in a moment of tolerable good humour, patched together a Gian Luigi Fiesco out of mouldering deserts? No, Leonora. I am too proud to accept as a gift what I can earn myself. Tonight I shall toss all this borrowed ornament back into the grave of my ancestors. --The *Counts* of Lavagna have died out. --*Princes* now begin.

LEONORA (*shakes her head, lost in fantasy*). I see my husband fall to the ground, mortally wounded-- (*Her voice more hollow.*) I see silent bearers bringing my husband's broken body toward me. (*Leaps up, startled.*) The first--the only ball flies through Fiesco's soul.

FIESCO (*takes her hand lovingly*). Calm yourself, my child. This single ball will do no such thing.

LEONORA (*regards him earnestly*). Fiesco tempts Heaven so confidently? And if it were the thousandth thousandth chance, it could still come true, and my husband would be lost. --Imagine you were wagering for Heaven, Fiesco. Even if there were a billion wins against one single miss, would you be bold enough to shake the dice and take up that impudent bet with God? No, my husband! When *everything* is at stake, every roll is blasphemy.

FIESCO (*smiling*). Do not worry. *I'm* on better terms with luck.

LEONORA. Do you say that--and were present at that mind-distorting game--what you call amusement--and watched faithless Fortune, how she lured her favourite with lucky little cards until he was warmed up, got to his feet, and bet the bank--and deserted him then in the throw of desperation. --My husband, you shall not go out to show yourself to the Genoese and be adulated. To rouse Republicans from their slumber, remind the steed that he has hooves, is no stroll in the park, Fiesco. Do not trust these rebels. The smart ones, who goaded you on, fear you; the stupid ones, who idolized you, are of little use to you, and wherever I look, Fiesco is lost.

FIESCO (*pacing with long strides*). Pusillanimity is the foremost danger. Greatness, too, exacts a price.

LEONORA. Greatness, Fiesco? --That your genius should be so ill-disposed toward my heart! --Let us say I trust your luck, that is, you prevail. --So much the worse for me, the most pitiful of my sex! Unhappy if it miscarries, unhappier still if it succeeds! There is no choice here, beloved. When he fails of the dukedom, Fiesco is lost. My husband is lost, when I embrace the Duke.

FIESCO. I don't understand.

LEONORA. You do, my Fiesco. At the stormy latitude of the throne the tender shoot of love dries up. The human heart, even Fiesco's, is too narrow for two almighty *gods—gods* who dislike each other so. *Love* has *tears* and can *understand* tears; *imperiousness* has eyes of brass, where no feeling pools. --*Love* has but *one* good, renounces all the rest of creation; *imperiousness* is ravenous even as it plunders all Nature. --*Imperiousness* hacks the world into a clanking house of chains; *love*, dreaming, finds its Elysium in every desert. --If you wanted to cradle yourself on my bosom now, an unruly vassal would come knocking at your kingdom. --If I wanted to throw myself into your arms now, your despot's fear would hear a murderer shuffling out from behind the tapestries and send you fleeing from room to room. Indeed, suspicion, all eyes, would infect our very household harmony in the end. --If your Leonora should now bring you refreshment, you would push away the goblet, shuddering, and scold loving tenderness for a mixer of potions.

FIESCO (*stands still, horrified*). Leonora, stop. This is hateful imagining--

LEONORA. But the picture isn't finished yet. I would say, sacrifice *love* to greatness, sacrifice *peace and quiet*--if only Fiesco remains. --God! That's the breaking point! --Rarely have angels ascended a throne, even *more* rarely have they descended from it again. One who need fear no man, will he take pity on any man? One who can arm every wish with a thunderbolt, will he deign to accompany it with a kind word? (*She pauses, then approaches him shyly and takes his hand; with exquisite bitterness.*) *Princes*, Fiesco? Those *botched projects* of Nature, who will, but cannot? --So pleased to *seat themselves* between the Human and the Divine: god-forsaken creatures, even worse creators.

FIESCO (*rushes about the room in agitation*). Leonora, stop. I've burnt my bridges--

LEONORA (*looks at him with longing*). How so, my husband? Only deeds are indelible. (*With melting tenderness and a bit roguish.*) I once heard you swear my beauty had brought down all your plans. --You swore falsely, you deceiver, or my beauty faded early. --Ask your heart who the guilty party is. (*More urgently, embracing him with both arms.*) Come back! Be a man! Give it up! Love will compensate you. Can my *heart* not still your monstrous hunger? --Oh, Fiesco, the *diadem* will be poorer still-- (*Coaxing.*) Come! I will learn all your desires by heart, will melt all the enchantments of Nature together into a single loving kiss, to hold this exalted fugitive forever in these heavenly bonds. --Your heart is endless. --Love is, too, Fiesco. (*Melting.*) To make a poor creature happy--a creature that finds its heaven on your bosom: ought that to leave an empty place in your heart?

FIESCO (*deeply shaken*). Leonora, what have you done? (*He falls helplessly into her arms.*) I will not come into the presence of another Genoese--

LEONORA (*in joyful haste*). Let us flee, Fiesco-- Let us toss away all this gaudy nothingness. Let us live only for love in meadows of romance. (*She presses him to her, enchanted.*) Our souls, as clear as the fair blue sky above us, will then no longer be tainted by the black breath of sorrow. --Our life will then flow melodically like a babbling spring toward the Creator-- (*The cannon sounds. Fiesco springs away. All the Conspirators enter the hall.*)

Scene 15

CONSPIRATORS. The time has come!

FIESCO (*to Leonora, firmly*). Farewell! Forever--or tomorrow Genoa lies at your feet.[60] (*About to rush out.*)

BOURGOGNINO (*cries*). The Countess is collapsing. (*Leonora in a faint. All rush to support her. Fiesco on his knees before her.*)

FIESCO (*very urgently*). Leonora! Help! For God's sake! Help! (*Rosa, Bella come to bring her around.*) She's opening her eyes-- (*He leaps up, resolute.*) Then come--to close Doria's. (*The Conspirators rush from the hall.*)

(*Curtain.*)

Act Five

After midnight. Broad street in Genoa. Lamps burn here and there at a few houses, then go out one by one. In the background, the St. Thomas Gate, still closed. In the distance, the sea. A few figures cross the square, carrying closed lanterns; then the Watch and a Patrol. Everything is quiet. Only the sea laps somewhat noisily.

Scene 1

Fiesco enters, armed, and stops before the palace of Andrea Doria; then Andrea.

FIESCO. The old man has kept his word. --All lights out in the palace. The guard is gone. I'll ring. (*Rings.*) Hey! Holla! Wake up, Doria! Betrayed, sold-out Doria, wake up! Holla! Holla! Holla! Wake up.

ANDREA (*appears on the terrace*). Who pulled the bell?

FIESCO (*his voice altered*). Don't ask. Obey. Your star is setting, Duke. Genoa is rising against you. Your hangmen are at hand, and you can sleep, Andrea?

ANDREA (*with dignity*). I remember how the angry sea quarrelled with my *Bellona*,[61] so that the keel groaned and the topmost mast broke--and Andrea Doria slept soundly. Who is sending these hangmen?

FIESCO. A man more terrible than your raging sea. Gian Luigi Fiesco.

ANDREA (*laughs*). You're in fine humour, friend. Bring us your little comedies by day; midnight is an unaccustomed hour.

FIESCO. You're making fun of the man who warns you?

ANDREA. I thank him and return to bed. Fiesco has revelled himself drowsy and has no time to spare for Doria.

FIESCO. Unhappy old man-- Don't trust the snake. Seven colours tangle on its glistening back--you approach--and suddenly the deadly coil has snared you. You laughed off a hint by a traitor. Do not laugh off the counsel of a friend. A horse is standing saddled in your courtyard. Flee while there's still time. Don't laugh off a friend.

ANDREA. Fiesco thinks nobly. I have never offended him, and he will not betray me.

FIESCO. Thinks nobly, will betray you, and has given you examples of both.

ANDREA. Then there's the *bodyguard*, which no Fiesco can overcome, unless cherubim serve under him.

FIESCO (*dismissive*). I'd like to have a word with them, to post a letter into Eternity.

ANDREA (*grandly*). You poor scoffer! Have you never heard that *Andrea Doria is eighty years old and Genoa--happy*? (*He leaves the terrace.*)

FIESCO (*looking after him in admiration*). Did I have to *overthrow* this man before I learn that it is harder yet to equal him? (*He walks up and down, reflecting.*) Well! I have matched greatness against greatness. --We are quit, Andrea. And now, destruction, take your course.

(*He rushes into the farthest lane. Drums sound on all sides. Sharp skirmish at the St. Thomas Gate. The gate is sprung and opens the prospect onto the harbour, where ships lie at anchor, lit by torches.*)

Scene 2

Gianettino Doria, wrapped in a scarlet cloak. Lomellino. Preceded by Servants carrying torches. All in haste.

GIANETTINO (*comes to a halt*). Who ordered the alarm sounded?

LOMELLINO. A cannon boomed on the galleys.

GIANETTINO. The slaves will be breaking their chains. (*Shots at the St. Thomas Gate.*)

LOMELLINO. Firing there.

GIANETTINO. The gate open. The guard in uproar. (*To the Servants.*) Quick, rascals. Light the way to the harbour. (*They hurry toward the gate.*)

Scene 3

As above. Bourgognino with Conspirators coming from the St. Thomas Gate.

BOURGOGNINO. Sebastiano Lescaro is a gallant soldier.

CENTURIONE. Defended himself like a bear until he fell.

GIANETTINO (*steps back, aghast*). What was that? --Halt!

BOURGOGNINO. Who goes there with the torch?

LOMELLINO. Enemies, Prince. Slip away here to the left.

BOURGOGNINO (*challenges heatedly*). Who goes there with the torch?

CENTURIONE. Stop! The password!

GIANETTINO (*draws defiantly*). Submission and Doria.

BOURGOGNINO (*furious and terrible*). Ravisher of the Republic and of my bride! (*To the Conspirators as he leaps upon Gianettino.*) Spared us an armed exchange, brothers. His very devils deliver him to us. (*He runs him through.*)

GIANETTINO (*falls bellowing*). Murder! Murder! Murder! Avenge me, Lomellino.

LOMELLINO, SERVANTS (*fleeing*). Help! Murderers! Murderers!

CENTURIONE (*calls with a strong voice*). He's hit. Stop the Count. (*Lomellino is captured.*)

LOMELLINO (*kneeling*). Spare my life-- I'll come over to you!

BOURGOGNINO. Is this monster still alive? Let the coward run. (*Lomellino escapes.*)

CENTURIONE. The St. Thomas Gate ours! Gianettino cold! Run as fast as you can. Report it to Fiesco!

GIANETTINO (*raises himself in paroxysm*). The pox! Fiesco. (*Dies.*)

BOURGOGNINO (*pulls the sword from the corpse*). Genoa free and my Berta--Your sword, Centurione, and bring this bloody one to my bride. Her prison has been sprung. I will come after and give her the bridegroom's kiss. (*They rush away to different sides.*)

Scene 4

Andrea Doria. German Soldiers.

GERMAN. The storm has moved off that way. Throw yourself in the saddle, Duke.

ANDREA. Let me look once more on Genoa's towers and the heavens. No, this is no dream, and Andrea is betrayed.

GERMAN. Enemies on all sides. Away! You can curse them when you're over the frontier!

ANDREA (*throws himself on his nephew's corpse*). Here is where I want to end. Let no one speak of flight. Here lies the strength of my old age. My journey is over. (*Calcagno appears in the distance with Conspirators.*)

GERMAN. Murderers there! Murderers! Flee, old Prince.

ANDREA (*as the drums begin again*). Hear that, Germans! Hear that! That's the Genoese, whose yoke I broke. (*Covers his face.*) Is that the thanks they show in your country, too?

GERMAN. Away! Away! Away! While our German bones put notches in their blades. (*Calcagno closer.*)

ANDREA. Save yourselves! Leave me here! Shock the nations with your hideous news: The Genoese struck down their father--

GERMAN. Murder! It'll be a while before the slaughtering starts. --Comrades, stand! Take the Duke into your midst. (*They draw.*) Whip some respect for a grey head into these Latin dogs--

CALCAGNO (*challenges*). Who goes there? What's going on?

GERMANS (*clashing*). German swords! (*They go off fighting. Gianettino's corpse is carried off.*)

Scene 5

Leonora in men's clothing. Arabella following her. Both creep out anxiously.

ARABELLA. Come, my Lady. Oh, do come--

LEONORA. The uproar's raging off in that direction. --Hark! Wasn't that a death cry? --Alas! They're closing on him. --Their gaping barrels point at Fiesco's heart. --At mine, Bella. --They let fire. --Halt! Halt! That's my husband. (*She throws up her arms, transported.*)

ARABELLA. For the love of God--

LEONORA (*still fantasizing wildly, crying in all directions*). Fiesco! --Fiesco! --Fiesco! --They're falling away in his rear, his loyalists. --Rebel loyalty is inconstant. (*Loudly, startled.*) My husband leading rebels? Bella? Heavens! My Fiesco fighting as a rebel?

ARABELLA. Oh, no, Signora, but as Genoa's terrible arbiter.

LEONORA (*attentively*). Now that would be something. --And Leonora trembled? The First Republican embraced by the most cowardly of republican women? --Go, Arabella. --When men match themselves for whole nations, women, too, take heart. (*The drums begin again.*) I'll join the fighters.

ARABELLA (*with despairing handclap*). Merciful heaven!

LEONORA. Wait! What have I stumbled on? Here's a hat and a cloak. And a sword, too. (*She weighs it.*) A heavy sword, my Bella, but surely I can drag it, and a sword does not disgrace its bearer. (*Storm is sounded.*)

ARABELLA. Do you hear? Do you hear? That's wailing from the Dominicans' tower. God have mercy! How frightful!

LEONORA (*fantasizing*). No, how delightful! In this storm signal my Fiesco is speaking to Genoa. (*Drums become louder.*) Hurrah! Hurrah! Flutes never sounded so sweet. --My Fiesco speaks also in these drums. --How my heart beats higher! All Genoa awakes. --Mercenaries spring to his banner, and his wife should be faint-hearted? (*Storm sounds on three other towers.*) Oh, no. A heroine will embrace my hero. --My Brutus is to embrace a Roman woman. (*She dons the hat and throws the mantle around her.*) I am Portia.

ARABELLA. My Gracious Lady, you don't know how dreadfully you are raving. No, you do not know. (*Storm bells and drums.*)

LEONORA. Poor soul, to hear all that and *not* rave! These stones could *weep* that they have no legs to leap to my Fiesco's side. --These palaces are angry at their masters, who planted them so firmly in the ground that they cannot spring to my Fiesco's side. --The embankment, if it could, would lay down its duty, abandon Genoa to the sea, and go to dance behind his drum. --Something that shakes Death from its winding sheet cannot raise your spirits? Go! --I will find my way.

ARABELLA. Dear God! You're not going to try to realize this madness?

LEONORA (*proud and heroic*). I should think so, you silly-- (*Fiery.*) When the uproar rages wildest, where my Fiesco fights in person-- Is that Lavagna, I hear them ask--whom no one can overcome, who throws iron dice for the prize of Genoa, is that Lavagna? --Genoese, I shall say, it is, and this man is my husband, and I, too, have a wound.[62]

(*Sacco enters with Conspirators.*)

SACCO (*challenges*). Who goes there? Doria or Fiesco?

LEONORA (*exalted*). Fiesco and Freedom! (*She throws herself into a lane. A throng surges over the scene. Bella is crowded back.*)

Scene 6

Sacco with a Pack of fighting men. Calcagno meets him with another Pack.

CALCAGNO. Andrea Doria has fled.

SACCO. That won't recommend you to Fiesco.

CALCAGNO. Like bears, those Germans. They planted themselves in front of the old man like a blank wall. I never even caught sight of him. Nine of ours are down. I took a glancing blow on the left earlobe. If they'll do *that* for *foreign* tyrants, what the devil won't they do to protect *their own princes*?

SACCO. We've collected a huge following and taken all the gates.

CALCAGNO. I hear there's heavy fighting around the Citadel.

SACCO. Bourgognino is among them. What's Verrina doing?

CALCAGNO. Lying between Genoa and the sea like the Hound of Hell, so that hardly an anchovy can get through.

SACCO. I'll start a storm beyond the walls.

CALCAGNO. I'll march over the Piazza Sarzano.[63] Get a move on, drummer. (*They march on to drums.*)

Scene 7

The Moor. A band of Thieves with fuses.

MOOR. So that you know, rascals. *I'm* the one who thickened this soup. --And then they won't give me a spoon. Well and good. A hunt suits me just fine. We'll give them a round of fire and plunder. Over there they're throwing punches for a dukedom; we're going to stoke the churches so that the freezing apostles can warm up again. (*They break into the adjacent houses.*)

Scene 8

Bourgognino. Berta disguised.

BOURGOGNINO. Rest here, little one. You're out of danger. Are you bleeding?

BERTA (*her speech altered*). No, not at all.

BOURGOGNINO (*vividly*). Fie! Then get up. I want to bring you where they're taking wounds for Genoa. --Fine ones, don't you see, like this one. (*He pushes back a sleeve.*)

BERTA (*starting back*). Heavens!

BOURGOGNINO. You're horrified? You little thing, you've rushed into manhood too early. --How old are you?

BERTA. Fifteen.

BOURGOGNINO. Not good. Five years too tender for a night like this. --Your father?

BERTA. The best citizen in Genoa.

BOURGOGNINO. Not so fast, boy. There's only *one*, and his daughter is my betrothed bride. Do you know the house of Verrina?

BERTA. I should think so.

BOURGOGNINO (*quickly*). And do you know his divine daughter?

BERTA. Berta is her name.

BOURGOGNINO (*urgently*). Go straight there and bring her this ring. Tell her it's for a wedding ring, and the man with the blue plume is doing fine. Farewell, then. I'm headed that way. The danger hasn't passed yet. (*Several houses are burning.*)

BERTA (*calls after him in a soft voice*). Scipio!

BOURGOGNINO (*stands still, surprised*). Oh, my sword! I know that voice--

BERTA (*falls into his arms*). Oh, my heart! You know it very well.

BOURGOGNINO (*cries*). Berta! (*Storm is sounded beyond the walls. A throng. They lose themselves in an embrace.*)

Scene 9

Fiesco enters in hot temper. Cibo. Followers.

FIESCO. Who set these fires?

CIBO. The Citadel is taken.

FIESCO. Who set these fires?

CIBO (*signals his followers*). Patrols after the offender! (*A few go off.*)

FIESCO (*angrily*). Do they want to make me out to be an arsonist? Buckets and spray right away! (*Followers go off.*) And Gianettino has been taken?

CIBO. That's what they say.

FIESCO (*wild*). They *say*? Who only *says* that? Cibo, by your honour, has he escaped?

CIBO (*hesitating*). If I can set the witness of my eyes against the witness of a nobleman, Gianettino lives.

FIESCO (*explosive*). You're talking your head into a noose, Cibo!

CIBO. To repeat-- I saw him alive eight minutes ago, a *yellow crest and scarlet cloak*.

FIESCO (*beside himself*). By all the gods! --Cibo! --I'm going to have Bourgognino shortened by a head. --Run, Cibo. --They're to bar every city gate--shoot every felucca to bits--block his escape by sea. --This diamond, Cibo, the finest in Genoa, Lucca, Venice, and Pisa. --The one who brings the news, *Gianettino is dead*--he shall have this diamond. (*Cibo rushes off.*) Run, Cibo.

Scene 10

Fiesco. Sacco. The Moor. Soldiers.

SACCO. We caught the Moor throwing a burning fuse into the Jesuit Cathedral--

FIESCO. I let your perfidy pass because it was aimed at *me*. Arson gets the rope. Take him away. String him up at the church door.

MOOR. Foo! Foo! Foo! I find that inconvenient. --Can't we arrange a little commutation?

FIESCO. None.

MOOR (*confidentially*). Then try sending me to the galleys.

FIESCO (*signals the others*). To the gallows.

MOOR (*resisting*). I'll turn Christian.

FIESCO. The Church declines your heathen pox.

MOOR (*wheedling*). Then at least send me soaked into Eternity.

FIESCO. Sober.

MOOR. But don't hang me on any Christian church.

FIESCO. A knight keeps his word. I promised you your own gallows.

SACCO (*growls*). No more dawdling, you heathen. We have other things to do.

MOOR. But--suppose the cord snaps?

FIESCO (*to Sacco*). We'll double it.

MOOR (*resigned*). So be it. --And the Devil can equip himself for a special case. (*Off, with Soldiers, who hang him in the distance.*)

Scene 11

Fiesco. Leonora enters at the back in Gianettino's scarlet cloak.

FIESCO (*becomes aware of her, moves forward, moves back, and murmurs grimly*). Don't I know that crest and cloak? (*Hurries closer, excited.*) I know that crest and cloak! (*Furious. Falls upon her and strikes her down.*) If you have three lives, stand up *again* and walk. (*Leonora falls with a broken sound. Victory march. Drums, horns, oboes.*)

Scene 12

Fiesco. Calcagno. Sacco. Centurione. Cibo. Soldiers appear with music and banners.

FIESCO (*meets them in triumph*). Genoese-- The die is cast. --Here he lies, who ate my soul--and fed my hatred. Raise your swords high! --Gianettino!

CALCAGNO. And I come to tell you that two-thirds of Genoa have taken your side and pledge allegiance to the banner of the Fieschi--

CIBO. And by me Verrina sends greetings from the admiral's ship and mastery of harbour and sea--

CENTURIONE. And by me the Governor of the city his commandant's baton and the keys--

SACCO. And in me (*kneels*) the Grand and Minor Council of the Republic[64] throw themselves at the feet of their master and beg for mercy and forbearance--

CALCAGNO. Let me be the first to bid the great victor welcome within his walls. --Hail to you--dip the flags--*Duke of Genoa!*

ALL (*remove their hats*). *Hail! Hail to the Duke of Genoa!* (*Military march.*)

FIESCO (*has stood the while, his head sunk onto his breast in an attitude of reflection*).

CALCAGNO. The people and the Senate stand waiting to greet their Gracious Lord in princely state. --May Your Grace permit us to bear you in triumph to the Signoria.

FIESCO. First let me do justice to my heart. --I had to leave a certain cherished person behind in anxious presentiment, one who will share with me the glory of this night. (*Moved, to the Company.*) Be so good as to accompany me to your amiable *Du*chess. (*About to depart.*)

CALCAGNO. Is this villainous assassin to lie here and dissemble his vileness in a corner?

CENTURIONE. Mount his head on a halberd!

CIBO. Let his dismembered rump sweep our cobblestones. (*Light is thrown on the corpse.*)

CALCAGNO (*shocked, quietly*). Look here, Genoese. That, in God's name, is no face of Gianettino's. (*All stare blankly at the corpse.*)

FIESCO (*comes to a stop, throws a searching glance sidelong, then withdraws it slowly, frozen and grimacing*). No. The devil-- No. That's no face of Gianettino's. Oh, you grinning devil! (*Rolling his eyes.*) Genoa *mine*, you say? Mine? (*A burst of rage, a terrible cry.*) Hell's own deception! It's my wife. (*Sinks to the ground, thunderstruck.*)

(*Conspirators stopped dead, gathered in shuddering groups.*)

FIESCO (*weakly propped up, muffled voice*). Have I murdered my wife, Genoese? --I beg you, don't cast such ghastly sidelong glances at what

Nature's playing here. God be praised! There are fates no *man* need fear, because he is *but human*. One denied the beatitude of the gods will know no devil's torment. --And this aberration would be yet worse. (*With terrible calm.*) Thank God, Genoese, this cannot be.

Scene 13

As above. Arabella enters, wailing.

ARABELLA. Let them kill me. What more have I to lose? --Have mercy, you men. Here I was separated from my Gracious Lady, and I cannot find her anywhere.

FIESCO (*approaches her; with faint, trembling voice*). Your Gracious Lady is called Leonora?

ARABELLA (*pleased*). Oh, *you're* here, my dear Gracious Master. --Don't be angry with us; we couldn't stop her any more.

FIESCO (*with suppressed rage*). You wretch! Stop her from what?

ARABELLA. From running after--

FIESCO (*more violent*). Silence! After what?

ARABELLA. In among the throng--

FIESCO (*furious*). And your tongue turn into a crocodile-- Her dress?

ARABELLA. A scarlet cloak--

FIESCO (*lunging at her*). Into the ninth circle of Hell[65] with you! The cloak--?

ARABELLA. Was lying on the ground here--

A FEW CONSPIRATORS (*murmur*). Gianettino was murdered here--

FIESCO (*staggers back, dull and exhausted; to Arabella*). Your Lady has been found. (*Arabella goes off, still fearful. Fiesco sweeps the crowd with a searching glance, then in a soft, hovering voice that rises gradually to frenzy.*) True it is. --Too true. --And I am the butt of this unbounded knavery. (*Striking out like a cornered animal.*) Back off, all you human faces. --Oh, (*insolently baring his teeth at the heavens*) if only I had *His* universe between my teeth.

--I feel like clawing all of Nature into a snarling beast, making it look like my pain. (*To those who stand around him shuddering.*) Lord! --How it stands there, this wretched breed, and crosses itself and congratulates itself that it is not like me. --Not like me! (*A hollow, trembling diminuendo.*) I alone have-- (*More rapid and wild.*) Me? Why me? Why not these, too, along with me? Why should I not be able to dull my pain on the pain of a fellow creature?

CALCAGNO (*fearful*). My esteemed Duke--

FIESCO (*bears down on him with cruel pleasure*). Oh, welcome! Here, thank God, is one whom this thunderbolt has also flattened! (*Embraces Calcagno furiously.*) Thunderstruck like me, my brother! Congratulations on your damnation! She is dead! *You*, too, loved her! (*He forces him down on the corpse and presses his head against it.*) Despair! She's dead! (*Staring to the side.*) Oh, that I stood at the gates of damnation, that my eye could look down shuddering on the manifold torture devices of purposeful Hell, my ear suck in the whimpering of crushed and contrite sinners! --If I could see it, my torment, who knows, would I then perhaps be able to bear it? (*Shuddering as he approaches the corpse.*) *My wife lies here, murdered.* --No. That says too little. (*With greater emphasis.*) *I, wretch, have murdered my wife.* --Pooh! That won't raise the pulse of Hell. --First it contrives to whirl me onto the highest, slipperiest, giddiest rooftop of joy, cajoles me onto the very doorstep of Heaven--and *then* plunges, then--oh, if only my breath could breathe the plague in among souls--then, then, I murder my wife. --No. Its malice is finer *yet*. --Then (*contemptuous*) two eyes fail to see, and (*with terrible emphasis*) I--murder--my wife! (*A biting laugh.*) That is the masterpiece.

(*All the Conspirators clutch their weapons, moved. Some wipe away tears. Pause.*)

FIESCO (*exhausted, more quietly, as he scans the circle*). Is anyone sobbing? --Yes, by God, *those who throttled a prince weep.* (*Melting into quiet sorrow.*) Speak! Are you weeping over death's high treason here or are you weeping over my mind's plunge headlong into unmanliness? (*Before the dead woman, grave and affecting.*) Where rock-hard murderers melt into warm tears, Fiesco's despair cursed and swore. (*Sinks down upon her, weeping.*) Leonora, forgiveness. --Rage won't bring repentance down from Heaven. (*Softly, sorrowfully.*) Years in advance, Leonora, I savoured the festive moment when I would bring the Genoese their Duchess. --I saw your cheeks redden with charming modesty; your bosom rise, princely and lovely, under the cloth of silver; heard your soft voice fail becomingly for joy. (*More vivid.*) Ha! With what intoxication the proud cheering swelled in my ears; how the triumph of my love was reflected in diminishing envy-- Leonora-- The moment has come. --Your Fiesco is Genoa's Duke. --And Genoa's most threadbare beggar would not give up his contempt in return for my torment and my scarlet. (*More touching.*) A wife shares one's sorrow. --*Who* will share my glory? (*He weeps harder and hides his face on the corpse. Compassion on all faces.*)

CALCAGNO. A most excellent noblewoman.

CIBO. Let us keep this bereavement from the people. It would take courage away from our friends and give it to our enemies.

FIESCO (*stands up, composed and firm*). Hear me, men of Genoa-- Providence, if I understand her gesture, struck this wound to test my heart for coming greatness? --It was the extreme of trials. --I now fear neither torment nor transport. Come. *Genoa awaits me,* you said? --I will give Genoa a prince such as no European has ever seen. --Come! --I shall give this unhappy princess such a funeral that life will lose its admirers, and decay take on the splendour of a bride. --Follow your Duke. (*All go off to a military march.*)

Scene 14

Andrea Doria. Lomellino.

ANDREA. They're going off that way with their cheering.

LOMELLINO. Their luck has gone to their heads. The gates are stripped of defenders. They're surging off toward the Signoria.

ANDREA. A horse that bolted only at my nephew. My nephew is dead. Listen, Lomellino--

LOMELLINO. What? *Still?* You *still* hope, Duke?

ANDREA (*gravely*). Fear for your life: to call me Duke is to *mock* me, if I can no longer *hope*.

LOMELLINO. My most Gracious Lord-- An erupting nation lies in the Fiesco side of the balance. --What lies in yours?

ANDREA (*grand and ardent*). Heaven itself.

LOMELLINO (*shrugging dismissively*). Now that powder's been invented, the angels no longer go bivouacking.

ANDREA. You pitiful ape, to deprive a despairing grey head also of its God. (*Grave and commanding.*) Go. Make it known that Andrea still lives. --Andrea, you will say, entreats his children not to drive him in his eightieth year out among strangers, who would never forgive him the loss of the flower of his fatherland. Tell them that. And that Andrea entreats of his children *so much* soil of his fatherland for *so many* bones.

LOMELLINO. I will obey, but I have no hope. (*About to go.*)

ANDREA. Hear me. Take this ice-grey lock of hair with you. --Say that it was the last one on my head and came loose in the third night of January, when Genoa tore loose from my heart, and had held for eighty years, and left my bald head in its eightieth year. --The lock of hair is brittle, but still strong enough to clasp the Purple of that *slender youth*. (*He goes off, covering his face. Lomellino hurries into a lane opposite. A tumultuous burst of joy, to trumpets and drums.*)

Scene 15

Verrina coming from the harbour. Berta and Bourgognino.

VERRINA. They're cheering. For whom?

BOURGOGNINO. They're probably proclaiming Fiesco Duke.

BERTA (*presses anxiously against Bourgognino*). My father is terrible, Scipio.

VERRINA. Let me be alone, children. --Oh, Genoa! Genoa!

BOURGOGNINO. The mob idolizes him and brayed for the Purple. The nobility watched, horrified, and was not in a position to say, No.

VERRINA. My Son, I have sold all my possessions and sent the gold on board your ship. Take your wife and set sail immediately. I may follow.

--Or I may not. Make for Marseille[66] (*oppressed, embracing them hard*), and God go with you. (*Rapid exit.*)

BERTA. For heaven's sake! What's my father contemplating?

BOURGOGNINO. Did you understand your father?

BERTA. To flee, oh, God. Flee in the wedding night!

BOURGOGNINO. That's what he said. --And we obey.

(They go toward the harbour.)

Scene 16

Verrina. Fiesco in ducal regalia. They run into one another.

FIESCO. Verrina! Excellent. I was just looking for you.

VERRINA. That was also my errand.

FIESCO. Does Verrina notice no change in his friend?

VERRINA (*reserved*). I wish none.

FIESCO. But do you find none?

VERRINA (*without looking at him*). I hope not. No.

FIESCO. I ask if you find none?

VERRINA (*after a fleeting glance*). I find none.

FIESCO. Well, you see, then it must be true that power does not make tyrants. Since we parted, I've become Genoa's Duke, and Verrina (*presses Verrina to him*) finds my embrace as warm as ever.

VERRINA. The greater the pity that I must return it coldly. The aspect of majesty falls like a whetted knife between me and the Duke! Gian Luigi Fiesco held great estates in my heart. --Now he has conquered Genoa, and I reclaim what is mine.

FIESCO (*startled*). God forbid. For a duchy *that* would be too Jewish a price.

VERRINA (*murmurs darkly*). Has freedom fallen so out of fashion that one tosses republics after just anyone?

FIESCO (*compresses his lips*). Say that to no one but Fiesco.

VERRINA. Oh, certainly. Only to an exceptional mind can one speak truth, unpunished. --But what a shame! Our clever card player erred with respect to *only one* card. He had calculated how *envy* would play its hand, but, too clever for his own good, failed to take account of the *patriots*. (*Very meaningful.*) Has the suppressor of freedom also kept in reserve a marked card to play against the hand of *Roman virtue*? I swear by the living God: Before posterity digs my bones out of the churchyard of a *duchy*, it will have to collect them from the *wheel*.

FIESCO (*takes him mildly by the hand*). Even if the Duke is your brother? If he only makes of his principality a treasure house of beneficence, neglected till now in domestic stinginess? Even then, Verrina?

VERRINA. Even then. --Booty freely given away has helped no thief down from the scaffold. This magnanimity, furthermore, is misaddressed to Verrina. I could let a fellow citizen do good things for me--that I could hope to reciprocate. The gifts of a prince are *grace*--and God alone is gracious to me.

FIESCO (*annoyed*). I'd more likely rip Italy from the Atlantic[67] than such obstinacy from its delusion!

VERRINA. And ripping is not the least of your arts. We could hear of that from the lamb of our Republic, which you have ripped from the gullet of that wolf Doria--only to gobble it up yourself. --But enough. Incidentally, Duke, tell me: What was the crime of that poor devil you had strung up on the Jesuit Cathedral?[68]

FIESCO. The rotter was putting Genoa to the torch.

VERRINA. But *that* rotter nonetheless spared the laws?

FIESCO. Verrina is torching my friendship.

VERRINA. So much for friendship. I tell you, I love you no longer; I swear to you that I hate you--hate you like the snake of Paradise, which made the first false throw in creation, for which the fifth millennium now bleeds. --Listen, Fiesco--I speak to you not as subject to master--not as friend to friend--but as *one human being to another*. (*Sharp and emphatic.*) You committed an outrage on the majesty of the one true God when you let virtue lend its hand to your knavery, when you let Genoa's patriots practice unchastity with Genoa. --Fiesco, if *I too* had been so benighted as *not* to notice this swindle, Fiesco! By all fear of Eternity, I would plait a rope of my own entrails and strangle myself, so that my escaping soul would spit gouty scum at you. Princely roguery surely buckles the gold balance that weighs human sin, but you have called out Heaven, and the Last Judgment will preside over your trial. (*Fiesco, astonished and speechless, measures him wide-eyed.*)

VERRINA. You needn't find an answer. We are quit. (*He walks up and down, then speaks.*) Duke of Genoa, aboard the ships of yesterday's tyrant I came to know a race of poor creatures who ruminate age-old guilt with every pull of the oars and weep their tears into an ocean that, like a rich man, disdains to count them. --A good prince inaugurates his regime by an act of mercy. Would you want to decide to free the galley slaves?

FIESCO (*sharply*). Let them be the first fruits of my tyranny. --Go announce their release to them all.

VERRINA. If you miss the expression of their joy, yours is but a half-done deed. Go yourself and see. Great lords are so seldom present when they do evil; are they also to do *good* things from ambush? --I should not think the Duke too grand for a beggar's sensibility.

FIESCO. You, sir, are terrible, but I don't know why I should obey. (*They go toward the sea.*)

VERRINA (*stops; with sadness*). *Embrace* me once more, Fiesco. There is no one here to see Verrina *weep* and have feeling for a prince. (*He presses him close.*) Surely two greater hearts never beat as one. We loved one another like brothers-- (*Weeping freely on Fiesco's shoulder.*) Fiesco, Fiesco, you vacate a place in my heart that all humankind, multiplied three times over, will never fill again.

FIESCO (*very moved*). Be--my--friend.

VERRINA. Throw aside this hateful Purple, and I am. --The first prince was a murderer and introduced the Purple to hide the blotches of his deed in this blood-red colour. --Hear me, Fiesco-- I am a warrior and know little of wet cheeks. --These are my first tears, Fiesco. --Throw this Purple aside.

FIESCO. Be still.

VERRINA (*more pressing*). Fiesco-- Let all the crowns of the planet be laid down here as prize, all its tortures be laid down there as bugbear, I'm to kneel before a mortal man--I shall *not* kneel--Fiesco. (*He kneels.*) Never have I knelt before. --Throw this Purple aside.

FIESCO. Stand up, and don't annoy me anymore.

VERRINA (*resolute*). I'll stand up and not annoy you anymore. (*They are standing at the gangplank of a galley.*) The prince has precedence. (*They start across.*)

FIESCO. Why are you tugging at my cloak? --It's falling off.

VERRINA (*with terrible scorn*). When the Purple falls, the Duke must follow. (*Throws him into the sea.*)

FIESCO (*calls from the water*). Help, Genoa! Help! Help your Duke! (*Sinks.*)

Scene 17

Calcagno. Sacco. Cibo. Centurione. Conspirators. Folk. All hurried and anxious.

CALCAGNO (*shouts*). Fiesco! Fiesco! Andrea is back. Half of Genoa is rallying to Andrea. Where is Fiesco?

VERRINA (*firmly*). Drowned.

CENTURIONE. Who answers for this? Hell? Or the madhouse?

VERRINA. He *was* drowned, if that sounds better. --I am on my way to Andrea.

(*All stand in frozen groups.*)

(*Curtain.*)

Notes to the Text

1. Nam id facinus... 'For I consider this deed memorable primarily on account of the newness of the crime and of the peril.' The Roman historian Sallust writing of the conspiracy in 63 BC of L. Sergius Catilina.

2. Retz: See Introduction.

3. Robertson: See Introduction.

4. The Hamburg dramaturg: G. E. Lessing (1729-1781). The *Hamburg Dramaturgy*, a collection of reviews of plays performed on the German stage and containing discussions of general principles of drama, appeared between 1767 and 1769. Lessing argued that the dramatist should remain true to the essential features of characters as known from historical sources.

5. *Robbers*: Schiller's first play, *Die Räuber*, 1781. The hero Karl Moor rebels against his father and expresses his opposition to society through the formation of a band of robbers.

6. This is the only play by Schiller which has a list of *dramatis personae* containing details of their character and appearance. Schiller no doubt intended this to be helpful to a theatre director and actors.

7. ANDREA DORIA: Doria was not in fact Doge, or a Duke, of Genoa, though he had considerable prestige and power. French dominance of Genoa ended in 1522 with the defeat of Francis I of France at the hands of imperial troops, with Doria, who had previously been loyal to the French, taking Genoa by land and sea. From an old noble Genoese family, Doria had distinguished himself in naval service. The government of the Repulic of Genoa was elected from and by members of the noble families.

8. GIANETTINO DORIA: Gianettino was not in fact the nephew, but the grandson of Andrea Doria.

9. FIESCO: Gian Lugi Fieschi, b. 1523. See Introduction.

http://dx.doi.org/10.11647/OBP.0058.03

10. *old German style*: Plain and simple in contrast to the courtly attire of the Dorias.

11. MULEY HASSAN: The figure of the Moor is entirely Schiller's invention, though a similar name was to be found in his sources.

12. LEONORA: Leonore Cibo married Duke Fieschi in 1542, was dispossessed and banished from Genoa with her three-year-old son after the conspiracy.

13. Apollo... Antinous: The Apollo of Belvedere and the Belvedere Antinous (a copy of the statue of Hermes by Praxiteles) were admired in eighteenth-century Germany as models of male beauty and mentioned by Winckelmann in his *Thoughts on the Imitation of Greek Works in Painting and Sculpture* (*Gedanken über die Nachahmung der griechischen Werke in der Malerei und Bildhauerkunst*, 1755).

14. Fiesco's coming: Schiller may have originally intended Fiesco to enter at the end of this scene as some critics suggest; but the fact that it is Gianettino Doria and the Moor who do, may suggest that some scenes can be thought of as taking place simultaneously.

15. sequins: The sequin (zecchino) was a gold coin minted by the Republic of Venice from the thirteenth century onwards.

16. Father of the Fatherland: A title given to Andrea Doria.

17. silhouette: One of several anachronisms in the play; the silhouette was fashionable in the eighteenth century.

18. San Lorenzo: The Roman Catholic cathedral in the centre of Genoa, dedicated to Saint Lawrence.

19. Procurator: Retiring governors and doges were chosen to be procurators, who oversaw the finances and taxes of the town.

20. Signoria: The Signoria, the supreme body of government of Genoa, was composed of eight Governors and the Doge chosen by the Grand Council.

21. Lanterna: The main lighthouse of the city's port and symbol of Genoa, which stands 117m above sea level, rebuilt in 1543. Gianettino's yielding to bourgeois constraints on his lust is like the lighthouse of Genoa yielding to the sea shells thrown by small boys.

22. Cibo's noble daughter: i.e. Leonore Fiesco.

23. peninsula: Schiller may have mistakenly believed that Genoa was a peninsula or be attributing this view to the Moor, who is not the most reliable of characters.

24. twice seventy ears: Hassan apparently has 69 men to assist him, but may be exaggerating.

25. what did that old Roman do: An allusion to the story of Virginius as told by the Roman historian Livy. Virginius stabbed his daughter to save her from being ravished by the Decemvir Appius Claudius. Lessing famously alluded to the story in the final act of his play *Emilia Galotti* (1772).

26. Election week: The Procurators and Signori were elected twice yearly, the Senators in December and the Doge in January.

27. Coromandel: The Coromandel Coast, the southeastern coastal region of India. The tropical wood of the Coromandel Coast provided the boards for ship construction.

28. Appius Claudius: See above: 'what did that old Roman do.'

29. my chocolate: An anachronism; chocolate was introduced to Europe in the early seventeenth century.

30. The handkerchief is damp: Cf. Shakespeare *Othello* Act III, Scene 4.

31. coffee houses: An anachronism; coffee houses appeared for the first time in Europe outside the Ottoman Empire in the seventeenth century.

32. Hanswurst: The coarse and cunning figure of German comedies, particularly popular in the sixteenth and seventeenth centuries. Gottsched notoriously attempted to banish him from the German stage in the 1730s. By the time Schiller wrote *Fiesco* the figure was no longer in evidence. His characteristic mark was a bald head. Here, Fiesco is threatening to go from harmless foolery (the fool's cap) to truly dangerous mischief. The threat and the theatrical vocabulary anticipate his dramatic revelation of his purposes in Act II, Scene 18. It is an instance of the metaphorics of masking and unmasking, pretense and ostensible revelation, of playacting that pervades *Fiesco*.

33. Via Balbi: One of the main streets of Genoa.

34. the boy Octavius: Julius Caesar's nephew and adopted son, later called Augustus, whose accession marked the end of the Roman Republic and the beginning of the Empire.

35. Florentine Venus: The Venus de' Medici, a life-size Hellenistic marble sculpture depicting the Greek goddess of love Aphrodite. Garve thinks this is an anachronism, since it was first mentioned in 1584 (see Garve, 44). Schiller saw a copy of this statue in Mannheim.

36. Unrest once broke out among the citizens of the Animal Kingdom:

Schiller's play abounds with animal imagery. Fiesco's address to the artisans, an Aesopian fable in which he easily convinces them of the pitfalls of democracy and the necessity of choosing a leader, is clearly inspired by Shakespeare's use of the body politic metaphor, for example in *Coriolanus* (Act I, Scene 1), where Menenius calms the people with his Fable of the Belly.

37. criminal Rota: The highest appeals court for all judicial trials in the Catholic Church. The court was named Rota (after Ital. *ruota*, wheel) because the judges originally met in a round room to hear cases.

38. Nero: According to Suetonius, Nero set Rome alight, and while observing it sang a poem on the ruin of Troy in the tragic dress he used on the stage.

39. the Emperor Charles: The Holy Roman Emperor Charles V was in Heilbronn at this time. Schiller has possibly used Bohemia to indicate that he was far away from Genoa.

40. black slate: Fiesco's name creates a double entendre: Ital. lavagna = slate.

41. Levant: An area on the coast to the West of Genoa.

42. Spinola: A member of a prominent noble family of Genoa mentioned in Schiller's sources; his role in Gianettino's plans in Schiller's play is unclear.

43. Darsena: Part of the inner harbour of Genoa.

44. Four galleys... Rome, Piacenza and France: Fiesco bought four galleys from the Pope and was in correspondence with the French ambassador in Rome. He also had the support of the Duke of Piacenza, the son of Pope Paolo III.

45. Loretto: The town of Loreto, a famous place of pilgrimage, inland from the Adriatic coast in the Marches region of central Italy.

46. beards of the circumcised: The circumcised are the Muslims, that is, the Turks, against whom Fiesco is supposedly fighting.

47. Endymion, chaste Luna: The shepherd prince Endymion, son of Zeus, was loved by the moon-goddess Selena (Luna) who descended nightly from heaven to consort with him.

48. Brutus: The reference may be to Marcus Junius Brutus, the assassin of Julius Caesar or to his ancestor, the founder of the Roman Republic, Lucius Junius Brutus.

49. Virginia and Appius Claudius: See above, Act I, 'what did that old Roman do.'

50. Eternal Liar: The Devil; Jn 8, 44.

51. my little Bononi: The Moor is referring to Diana Bononi (see Act II, Scene 15); The count in question is Lomellino. He came to Diana in the night, as Fiesco had said he would (II, 15), and paid for his pleasure by losing the list he had made for Gianettino and that he was carrying on Gianettino's instructions (II, 14). Bribed by the Moor, acting for Fiesco, Diana stole that list in the course of the night and gave it to the Moor, who now brings it to Fiesco.

52. the peace between France and Spain: The treaty of Crépy concluded by Holy Roman Emperor Charles V and King Francis I of France at Crépy-en-Laonnois on 18 September 1544 left mercenaries that Fiesco wished to employ idle.

53. Patroclus, too, had to die. Spoken by Achilles to Lycaon, King Priam's son, whom he is about to slay. Patroclus was Achilles' friend, whom Hector slew, prompting Achilles to return to battle and eventually to destroy Hector. *Iliad*, XXI, 107.

54. Sauli, Gentili, Vivaldi, and Vesodimari: Noble families of Genoa.

55. St. Thomas Gate: La Torre di San Tommaso, one of the tower gates on the wall of Genoa, dating from the fourteenth century.

56. fools on the banks of Acheron: Those sitting on the banks of the Acheron, one of the rivers leading to the Greek underworld, waiting to be ferried across by Charon.

57. Sebastiano Lescaro: A person so-named (or Lercaro) appears in Schiller's sources as an accomplice of Gianettino Doria.

58. flesh made of cast iron: Homer, *Iliad*, IV, 510.

59. the Triple Crown: The Papal Crown or Tiara; Fiesco is referring to his ancestors Pope Innocence III (1443-54) and Pope Adrian V (1276).

60. Genoa lies at your feet: Verbatim from Robertson's history.

61. Bellona: The ship on which Andrea Doria commanded several expeditions as imperial admiral.

62. I, too, have a wound: Cf. Portia in Shakespeare's *Julius Caesar*, Act II, Scene 2. Leonore continues to liken herself to Caesar's wife, whom she mentions explicitly beforehand.

63. Piazza Sarzano: One of the principle piazzas in the centre of Genoa.

64. The Grand and Minor Council of the Republic: Il Consiglio Grande and il Consiglio Minore. See above, Signoria. The Minor Council, consisting of 100 persons, was chosen by and from members of the Grand Council.

65. Ninth Circle of Hell: In Dante's *Inferno*, the deepest part of Hell for the worst sinners.

66. Marseille: Verrina, Calcagno and Sacco were banished from Genoa and sailed for Marseille.

67. Atlantic: Schiller wrote: 'Atlantenmeer,' the Atlantic Sea. The figure turns on the unlikelihood of lifting Italy from the Atlantic Sea. Whether Schiller in fact believed that Italy lay in the Atlantic Ocean is an open question.

68. Jesuit Cathedral: The Chiesa del Gesù e dei Santi Ambrogio e Andrea, a former Jesuit church near the Palazzo Ducale in Genoa.

Select Bibliography

Primary sources

Schiller, Friedrich von. *Schillers Werke*. Nationalausgabe. Ed. Julius Petersen et al. 42 vols. (Weimar: Herman Böhlaus Nachfolger, 1943-). Vol. 4 *Fiesco*, ed. Edith and Horst Nadler, 1983.

Schiller, Friedrich von. *Schillers Werke und Briefe*. Ed. Otto Dann et al. 12 vols. (Frankfurt: Deutscher Klassiker Verlag, 1988-2004). Vol. 2 *Dramen I*, ed. Gerhard Kluge, 1988.

Secondary sources

Blumenthal, Liselotte. 'Aufführungen der *Verschwörung des Fiesko zu Genua* zu Schillers Lebzeiten (1783-1805).' *Goethe. Neue Folge des Jahrbuchs der Goethe-Gesellschaft* 27 (1995), 60-90.

Craig, Charlotte. 'Fiesco's Fable: A Portrait in Political Demagoguery.' *Modern Language Notes 86* (1971): 393-399. http://dx.doi.org/10.2307/2907815

Fowler, Frank M. 'Schiller's *Fiesco* Re-examined.' *Publications of the English Goethe Society* N. S. 40: 1-29.

Grawe, Christian. *Friedrich Schiller. Die Verschwörung des Fiesko zu Genua. Erläuterungen und Dokumente*. Stuttgart: Reclam, 1985.

Guthrie, John. *Schiller the Dramatist. A Study of Gesture in the Plays* (Rochester, NY: Camden House, 2009).

Guthke, Karl S. *Schillers Dramen. Idealismus und Skepsis*. 2nd expanded and revised edn (Tübingen: Edition Orpehus, 2005).

Hinderer, Walter. '"Ein Augenblick Fürst hat das Mark meines ganzen Daseins verschlungen". Zum Problem der Person und der Existenz in Schillers.' *Verschwörung des Fiesko. Jahrbuch der deutschen Schillergesellschaft* 14 (1970): 230-273.

Janz, Rolf-Peter. 'Die Verschwörung des Fiesko zu Genua.' In *Schillers Dramen. Neue Interpretationen*. Ed. Walter Hinderer (Stuttgart: Reclam, 1983), pp. 37-57.

Kleinschmidt, Erich. 'Brüchige Diskurse: Orientierungsprobleme.' In Friedrich Schillers *Die Verschwörung des Fiesko zu Genua*. *Jahrbuch des Freien Deutschen Hochstifts* (2001): 100-121.

Lützeler, Paul M. 'Die große Linie zu einem Brutuskopf. Repblikanismus und Cäsarismus in Schillers *Fiesco*.' *Monatshefte* 70 (1978): 15-28.

Luserke-Jacqui, Matthias. *Friedrich Schiller* (Tübingen, Basel: Francke, 2005).

Mainland, William F. *Schiller and the Changing Past* (London: William Heinemann Ltd, 1957). Ch. 1.

Mücke, Dorothea von. 'Play, power and politics in Schillers 'Die Verschwörung des Fiesko zu Genua' *Michigan Germanic Studies* 13 (1987): 1-18.

Phelps, Reginald. 'Schiller's Fiesco – A Republican Tragedy?' *PMLA* 89 (1974): 442-453. http://dx.doi.org/10.2307/461580

Schiller-Handbuch. Leben, Werk, Wirkung. Ed. Matthias Luserke-Jacqui (Stuttgart: Metzler, 2005).

Wischnewsky, Michael. 'Betting on Providence: "Die Verschwörung des Fiesko zu Genua"' *Colloquia Germanica* 35 (2002): 27-58.

Wölfel, Kurt. 'Pathos und Problem. Ein Beitrag zur Stilanalyse von Schillers *Fiesko*.' *Germanische-Romanische Monatschrift*. N. F. 7 (1957): 224-244.

This book need not end here...

At Open Book Publishers, we are changing the nature of the traditional academic book. The title you have just read will not be left on a library shelf, but will be accessed online by hundreds of readers each month across the globe. We make all our books free to read online so that students, researchers and members of the public who can't afford a printed edition can still have access to the same ideas as you.

Our digital publishing model also allows us to produce online supplementary material, including extra chapters, reviews, links and other digital resources. Find *Fiesco's Conspiracy at Genoa* on our website to access its online extras. Please check this page regularly for ongoing updates, and join the conversation by leaving your own comments:

http://www.openbookpublishers.com/isbn/9781783740420

If you enjoyed this book, and feel that research like this should be available to all readers, regardless of their income, please think about donating to us. Our company is run entirely by academics, and our publishing decisions are based on intellectual merit and public value rather than on commercial viability. We do not operate for profit and all donations, as with all other revenue we generate, will be used to finance new Open Access publications.

For further information about what we do, how to donate to OBP, additional digital material related to our titles or to order our books, please visit our website: http://www.openbookpublishers.com

Knowledge is for sharing

www.ingramcontent.com/pod-product-compliance
Lightning Source LLC
Chambersburg PA
CBHW071214160426
43196CB00012B/2293